WORLDVIEW

WORLDVIEW

The Autobiography of a
Social Studies Teacher and Quaker

by
Leonard S. Kenworthy

Richmond, Indiana

Published by
Friends United Press
Richmond, IN

WORLDVIEW

1. Kenworthy, Leonard Stout, 1912-
2. Social scientists — United States — Biography.
3. Educators — United States — Biography. 4. Friends in the United
States — Biography. I. Title. H59.K45A38   300'.92'4 (B)
77-70183   ISBN 0-913408-27-1

Printed in the United States of America
by
Prinit Press, Dublin, Indiana

To My Family

Carroll and Mary Kenworthy
Wilmer and Frances Kenworthy
Tom and Suzan Kenworthy, Lane, Randy, Owen and
Lauren Eileen
Lee and Susan Kenworthy, Amy and Asa

PREFACE

Throughout my life I have read many autobiographies and biographies and have been struck by the fact that nearly all of them are about the famous — or the infamous. Often I have wished that there were more autobiographies of lesser lights — the inconspicuous rather than the conspicuous.

This autobiography is about one of those "lesser lights" — a person whose name has not made the headlines or the daily broadcasts or been featured in the mass circulation magazines. It is the story of a social studies teacher and college professor, a curriculum specialist, and a pioneer in the international dimension of education. It is an account of a short-time international civil servant and world traveler. And it is a report of the spiritual journey of an active Quaker.

But it is more than an autobiography. Several chapters are really essays about various organizations and movements, including an account of my part in them. This is especially true of the chapters on the progressive education movement, UNESCO, the civilian public service camps of World War II, the social studies movement and the international education movement, the Religious Society of Friends, and Quaker schools.

Writing such an autobiography is difficult but it is revealing and rewarding. People, places and events long buried in one's mind are uncovered and some of the patterns in one's life are more clearly seen than heretofore. In fact, writing an autobiography is so revealing that I wish everyone would do so, even if such an account is never published.

Several people urged me to write this account and I am grateful to them for their encouragement. They include Helen Hafner, Melvin Levison, Walter Mohr, Margaret Parke, Irene Vite, and my neighbors, Dr. and Mrs. Sam Morrock.

Several persons have also helped me to recall events

from the past, to remember the names of persons with whom I was associated, or to edit early drafts of various chapters. Among them were: Elton Atwater, Tom Brown, Jack Campbell, Clayton Farraday, Walter Mohr, Stuart Smith, and my brother Carroll Kenworthy. Despite strenuous efforts on my part to insure accuracy in names and dates, some errors have undoubtedly crept into this book. For such mistakes I beg the indulgence of readers.

Titles are difficult to decide upon. Some readers may be intrigued with this process and be interested in some of the titles considered. They included: A Lifetime of Learning and Teaching, Nudging Educators and Prodding Quakers, Expanding Horizons, Broadening Horizons, Promoting Pluralism, At Home on Planet Earth, and A Footnote to Educational History.

It is my hope that readers will enjoy this account of my life and that it will encourage them to reflect again on their sojourn on Planet Earth.

LEONARD S. KENWORTHY
BROOKLYN, NEW YORK

Contents

1   My Family and the World Around Me   1
2   Westtown School, Earlham College and
    Columbia University   17
3   My Earliest Attempts at Teaching — and
    Harvard Summer School   31
4   The Progressive Education Movement and
    the Eight Year Study at Friends Central
    School   41
5   Working for the American Friends Service
    Committee in Nazi Germany   57
6   Alternative Service in World War II; My
    Years in Civilian Public Service   73
7   The Religious Society of Friends and My
    Part in the Quaker Adventure   89
8   Helping To Create an International Edu-
    cational Organization: The Formation of
    UNESCO   105
9   Working on My Doctoral Degree and Taking
    Part in a Survey of Education in Puerto Rico   123
10 College Teaching and Two Nationally Signi-
    ficant Attempts To Improve Teacher
    Education   131
11 Helping Future Social Studies Teachers   149
12 88 Nations and 50 States — Travel Abroad
    and at Home   165
13 Visiting the New Nations and Interviewing
    Their Leaders   183
14 Encouraging American Educators To Teach
    About the World   195
15 Writing, Speaking, and Consulting with
    Schools   213
16 Textbooks as Scapegoats or as Many-
    Splendored Publications   227
17 Some Reflections on Quaker Schools   239
18 Semi-Retirement and Retirement — A Life-
    time of Learning and Teaching in Retrospect   255

WORLDVIEW

CHAPTER 1

My Family and the World Around Me

In the middle west of the U.S.A. in the 19th century the people in many villages and towns hoped that some major highway like the National Road would be routed through their community. Or they wanted a canal. Or they hoped for a railroad. If they could obtain one of those means of transportation, they were elated. Two would be wonderful. Acquiring all three was something to be sought, but almost impossible to achieve.

Richmond, Indiana, was one of the rare places which obtained all three. The National Road was routed through it and for a short time it had a canal. And in the 1850s it had railroad links with such cities as Chicago, Cincinnati, Dayton and Indianapolis.

Consequently Richmond grew. Originally it had been a small settlement of Quakers who had migrated from North Carolina, Ohio and Pennsylvania. They were frugal, industrious, God-fearing or God-loving people with their plain clothes and their *thees* and *thous*. They had a unique sense of community, too, with the Meeting House rather than the Town Hall as its center. Nearby was a Friends School, because Quakers considered the education of their children a necessity rather than a luxury. The Quakers also established a boarding school or secondary school in Richmond, and in 1859 that school

1

became Earlham College. By that time Richmond was a thriving city of over 6000 persons and the commercial and manufacturing center of a large agricultural area.

Early in the 19th century several persons in Richmond were also engaged in another "business" — helping slaves to escape from the south. The hub of that activity was a few miles north of Richmond where Levi Coffin, the so-called president of the Underground Railroad, and his wife Katie, lived.

Over the years other groups joined the Quaker community in Richmond, including Germans of both Lutheran and Catholic backgrounds, the Irish, and others. Together they helped to make Richmond a cosmopolitan city, far above average for that time.

It was in a plain white frame house which faced on the National Road that I was born on March 26, 1912, in the western part of Richmond. Perhaps the most important asset in life is the feeling of being wanted and from birth I was blessed with that asset.

The title of this introductory chapter was carefully chosen. It contains the words *me* and *my* because we are all egocentric when we are born. We are the center of the universe and the world revolves around us. The main task of life is to develop enough security in the *me* that it becomes *we*, gradually turning the egocentric child into the sociocentric adult.

My world, like the world of babies everywhere, was certainly circumscribed. At first it consisted of Mother, Dr. Ross, and the King sisters who helped mother until she was able to resume her role as co-head of the household. Gradually the male members of the family were discovered — my father, my brother Carroll, then age 8, and my brother Wilmer, age 4.

I am certain that there were other relatives who came on the scene soon as admiring onlookers — Grandmother Holloway from nearby Spiceland, a small Quaker community 30 miles to the west; and Grandpa and Grandma Kenworthy from New London, another small Quaker community a little over 100 miles northwest of Richmond. Eventually my world broadened and I saw,

2

then began to identify, and eventually to love Aunt Lou and Uncle Arthur Holloway and their children: Hazel, Ruth, Esther, Harold, Homer and Edna. And there were the Kenworthy aunt and uncle, Aunt Louie and Uncle Earl, and their children: Clarence, Paul, Mabel and Catherine.

Soon I acquired another aunt and uncle "by adoption" — Lieuetta and Elbert Russell. Uncle Elbert was the head of the biblical department at Earlham and Dad's "boss" and close friend. The Russells were near neighbors and their son and daughter, Josiah and Marcia, were playmates of my brothers.

All I knew about my mother (known as soon as I could talk as Mamma) was that she fed me, clothed me, sang to me, and loved me. Later in life I learned more about her. She had been born in Spiceland, Indiana. Her father was Asa Holloway, a successful farmer who provided his family with more than the usual amenities of life. He owned 90 acres of land, a large frame house with an elaborate chandelier with pendants, an attractive carriage, and fine horses. For their wedding trip he had taken his bride to Catalina Island in California, a long and expensive honeymoon. He also bought his wife an organ which Mamma learned to play. Asa Holloway was a good farmer and an active member of the Spiceland Friends Meeting. He died as a result of exposure to the cold when he was trying to protect his stock in a blizzard. Unfortunately for me, he died before I was born.

My mother's mother was a remarkable woman. She attended Spiceland Academy (a Quaker secondary school) and then the Quaker boarding school in Richmond before it became Earlham College. For several years she taught in various schools in eastern Indiana. Then, after the Civil War, she and her sister went south and helped to organize schools for Negro children, spending a year in Jackson, Mississippi, and two years in Helena, Arkansas. That was the equivalent in those days of taking part in the civil rights movement or Peace Corps. It was work sponsored by the Committee of Freedom of Indiana Yearly Meeting of Friends.

She married in her middle years and had four children, only two of whom lived — Arthur and Ida Lenora. Leaving her family in Spiceland for several months, she went to Chicago and enrolled in a course in homeopathic medicine, becoming one of the first women doctors in the middle west. Grandma Holloway played the organ, read widely, and sometimes wrote papers for various local groups. She was active in local church work and in temperance organizations. For years she served on the Board of Trustees of Spiceland Academy, the last of such Quaker schools in Indiana, being laid down in the 1920s.

So Mamma had a very good start in life. She came from "good people." She attended Spiceland Academy and Earlham College, where she was recognized as a talented singer. She also played the piano.

Mamma was an attractive as well as an able person — slender, with long jet-black hair and a dark complexion. She and Dad were both in the graduating class of 1900 at Earlham. In 1902 they were married and she took on the role of preacher's wife as well as wife and eventually mother. In her role as a minister's wife she did a great deal of entertaining of church groups and traveling dignitaries. She was also active in missionary societies, mothers' clubs, University Women's Clubs, and other organizations. Often she was an officer of such groups. But her husband and her family came first.

Her standards in speech, in appearance, and in morals were very high and she was demanding upon Dad, which was probably good for a young farmer turned public leader. She was also demanding of her sons, but extremely helpful to us, encouraging us in our school work, in our music, in our appearance, and in our behavior. She also helped us in speaking "pieces," which was the beginning of our interest in and training for the public speaking each of us has done throughout his life.

Dad's background was similar. He was born on a farm near New London, Indiana, just a few miles from Kokomo, the county seat of Howard County. Grandpa Kenworthy was a successful farmer and "retired" in his 40s, moving near New London and then into New

London but going out to his farm almost every day to help the hired man. Grandpa kept a horse and cow, chickens and bees, and had a small orchard and large garden. His father, Willis Kenworthy, had moved to New London so that his children could attend the Quaker school there. Grandpa had a few years of education, but never attended high school. His first wife was Hannah Stout (from whom I got my middle name), but she died early in life. Then he remarried, taking as his wife Lucy Newlin, an elementary school teacher in the community. They read together a great deal and in that way he was able to further his limited formal education.

The New London Friends Meeting had a paid minister during much of Grandpa's life, but a layman sat "at the head of Meeting" and Grandpa was that person for many years. He was also superintendent of the Sunday School, a Sunday School teacher for most of his life, treasurer of the Meeting for many years, the clerk of the Monthly and the Quarterly Meetings. In addition, he was a township trustee and a leader in almost all of the community's activities. In later years he and Grandma Kenworthy were generally known as "Uncle Mit" and "Aunt Lucy" and were prominent pillars of society.

Dad went to school in New London and graduated from the high school there. Then, due largely to his mother's interest and the influence of S. Edgar Nicholson, the principal of the local high school, he went on to Earlham College where he took his A.B. and M.A. degrees.

As a young man he had already begun to speak in the New London Friends Meeting and in 1897, at the age of 23, he was "recorded" as a minister, which meant that he had showed a special "gift" in the ministry. At Earlham he majored in religion and was tremendously influenced by Elbert Russell, the head of the biblical department.

After serving as pastor of Friends churches in Muncie, Paoli and Kokomo, Dad returned to Earlham in 1904 as a professor in the biblical department, staying there until 1908 when he entered the Harvard Divinity School, something unique in those days for a young Quaker minister in the middle west. From 1911 until 1915 he was back at Earlham, teaching at the college and serving as pastor of the West Richmond Friends Meeting.

At the time I was born he was a professor at the college. He had helped to build the house in which we lived and was understandably proud of it. It was almost directly across from the college and that made it convenient for him, his students and his faculty friends. I am sure that he and Mamma also felt that the college campus would make an ideal playground for their three sons.

Probably Dad and Mamma both thought in 1912 that they would remain at Earlham all or most of their lives. Dad had a good job at the college and at the West Richmond Friends Meeting. Richmond was a pleasant place in which to live and in which to raise a family. And the Holloway and Kenworthy relatives were not far away.

If that was their dream, it was soon shattered. Quakers are usually peaceful people. They have their disagreements, but they have ways of dealing with them which usually work remarkably well — sometimes miraculously. But when they don't use those methods, they have verbal battles which can be highly disruptive. Such a verbal battle broke out at Earlham just about the time I was born.

There are different versions of what happened. The one which Opal Thornburg related in her volume on *Earlham: The Story of a College,* focuses on a fight over whether a building for the new West Richmond Friends Meeting should be built on the Earlham campus. She stresses, too, the criticisms of President Robert Kelly as heavy-handed in his administration of the college. She acknowledges that there were also theological differences but downplays that aspect of the situation.

Another version emphasizes the centrality of the theological issues. At that point in history, new and revolutionary ideas were being promulgated throughout the United States, especially in colleges and universities. Some of them were political ideas, aspects of the Progressive Movement. Others were scientific ideas, and especially Darwinism and evolution, with many religious and educational implications. The idea of the "social gospel" was being promoted, too, with emphasis upon the here rather than the hereafter.

Quakers did not escape the tensions developed by such new ideas. Fresh winds were blowing and soon they attained hurricane proportions. Some older and "weighty" Friends were concerned about these ideas. They were basically fundamentalists who believed in the centrality of the Bible and in the literal interpretation of every passage in it. Such persons were sometimes concerned about social issues, but they were more concerned with salvation and sanctification, topics in which they were specialists. They did not like the new ideas which they felt were being taught at Earlham and they considered Elbert Russell a heretic and the chief culprit in a plot to alter the Society of Friends in the middle west by educating the younger generation in the new and pernicious beliefs which he and others espoused.

In such disputes there are almost always a variety of causes. That was certainly true in this conflict. No matter what the causes were, the conflict which ensued was long, involved, acrimonious and bitter. In a test of strength, the conservatives brought pressure on Dad to resign. Eventually he did so. Encouraged by their success, they then tackled Elbert Russell. In the end he submitted his resignation and it was accepted by the Board of Trustees "reluctantly."

Within a few years all four of the principals in that conflict had left Earlham — President Kelly and Professors Russell, Kenworthy and William Mendenhall. Each of them went on to serve with distinction elsewhere and fortunately for Earlham, each of them continued his support of the college.

In the coming years Dad served the Society of Friends in many capacities, and always with distinction. He was minister in several places, including Glens Falls, New York; Washington, D.C.; Amboy and Carthage, Indiana. He was executive secretary of Wilmington Yearly Meeting and Indiana Yearly Meeting. He was active in the American Friends Service Committee in various capacities. Likewise he was the first chairman of the

7

Friends Committee on National Legislation and of the Rural Life Association. He was one of the few midwestern Quakers who was known and respected in the east and served often as a bridge between those two groups.

After two years at Harvard, Dad completed his work for the Bachelor of Sacred Theology degree — the equivalent of a doctorate. Then we moved to Glens Falls, New York, where he was minister of the Friends Church. There had been difficulties in that group and he was called upon to act as a conciliator, a role he was to play several times and one which he always played well. It was at that time that Carroll went to Oakwood School, first in Union Springs and then in Poughkeepsie, New York. That was in the days when William Reagan was principal. And what a wonderful educator he was.

From Glens Falls, we moved to Wilmington, Ohio, where Dad became the executive secretary of Wilmington Yearly Meeting and taught some courses at Wilmington College. In his job with the yearly meeting, he was responsible for several small Meetings in the mountains of East Tennessee. In that task his farm background helped him, as most members of those mountain Meetings were trying to eke out a precarious existence from the poor and hilly soil. Dad saw possibilities for a new type of ministry and persuaded Edward and Daisy Ransome, New York Yearly Meeting Friends, to go south to establish a demonstration farm, and to work with the Meetings part-time.

One of my most memorable experiences was the summer Dad, Mamma and I spent in that part of Tennessee. It was really my first "foreign experience" as many of the people there were desperately poor and lived in log cabins. I recall staying in the only house in a large area which was constructed of planed boards, of making butter in an old-fashioned churn, and of trudging up and down a mountain to attend evening services, lanterns in hand in order to see our way. All this was a foretaste of my later experiences in developing nations.

Wilmington was a small town at that time, with approximately 5000 persons. Part of the time we lived on

8

the edge of the Wilmington College campus; later we moved to the center of the city. Carroll was in Earlham College at the time, a fact which distressed some Wilmington College people. But Wilmer and I knew Wilmington well, especially from trips here and there to sell the radishes and onions we had raised to earn pin money. We also sold tickets to the summer and winter Chautauquas in order to earn our own tickets to the series of concerts and lectures they included.

Then there was the Rodeheaver revival. And what an event that was for Wilmington. Homer Rodeheaver had worked with Billy Sunday as his choir director. Then he organized his own revival troupe. Several churches banded together and invited him to Wilmington. I don't recall a word he said and I was not one of those who were "saved." But Wilmer and I sang in the large children's choir, complete with such paraphernalia as flashlights to use in singing "Let the Lower Lights Be Burning," while the auditorium was darkened. And I remember the pianist and the flourishes as she ran her hands up and down the keyboard in the dramatic pauses in the chorus of "Love Lifted Me." The Rodeheaver revival didn't help my spiritual life, but what fun for a young boy in the 1920s in a small town.

I went to school in Wilmington and had a remarkable third-grade teacher named Carrie Ent, whom I have described briefly and affectionately in my book on *Social Studies for the Seventies*. School was apparently easy for me, judging by the report cards which my parents kept. In that third grade I received all A's except for writing. So that is where my abominable writing began! And in the fifth grade all A's — except deportment! I also took piano lessons at Wilmington College from a Mrs. Cadwallader. Years later I tried to figure out why I liked lemon pie so much and remembered that Mamma fed me hot lemon pie each Saturday before my piano lesson. What a practicing psychologist she was!

In 1921 Dad was asked by Wilbur Thomas, the head of the American Friends Service Committee, to go to the Soviet Union to direct the work there in famine relief. This was an opportunity for him to put his social gospel ideas into action and he went, leaving Mamma and two boys at home, and one son in college.

That was a long, lonesome, gruesome winter. I recall many a meal in which hominy was the chief dish, since it was inexpensive and we were trying to live simply on a Service Committee maintenance salary. Mamma read us Dad's letters — or parts of them — and I learned a little geography as well as about starving conditions in a foreign land. I also started a stamp collection, my first hobby.

Then, at Christmas, we received a cable from the Soviet Union. But it wasn't what we had expected. Instead of a message of love and Christmas cheer, it contained the news that Dad was seriously ill with typhus.

Fortunately for me, Grandma Holloway spent that winter with us in Wilmington. That was a boon, for I somehow sensed even then that she was someone very special. After dinner I would go to her room and we would read together. She called it "taking turns." She would read 10 pages or so and then I would read a page or two. In that way we devoured a small shelf of biographies from the public library. I suspect my lifelong interest in biography was launched then.

By spring Mamma was exhausted. She had had trouble with the drinking water in our well and difficulties with the farmer on the small farm we owned in Indiana. She had carried an even heavier load of family responsibilities than usual, even though Carroll had the family car and drove back and forth from Earlham to help her. She became ill in May and on the 23rd she died of peritonitis. I was 10 at the time and did not fully understand at first what had happened. But I learned. Oh, how I learned.

Carroll came home as soon as he learned about Mother's illness. Grandpa came. Uncle Earl and Uncle Arthur came. And the pastor of the Wilmington Friends Church and his wife, Earl and Clara O'Neil Harold, were extremely helpful. So were Elsie McCoy and others.

There were services in Wilmington and in New London, where Mamma was buried. Meanwhile a cable had been sent to Dad and he had begun his long, weary way home.

That summer was the first of several I spent with Grandpa and Grandma Kenworthy. I learned to hitch "Charley" to the spring wagon and to drive off with Grandpa to the farm. In the evening I went to the pasture land Grandpa owned and drove "Buttercup" back to the barn. And while Grandpa milked, I carried water for Grandma's endless beds of flowers, which I really liked, even though I thought they were too numerous. Nevertheless this was probably the beginning of my lifelong love of flowers.

Then Grandma and I sat on the old-fashioned settee on the front porch and talked — or just rocked. Sometimes she taught me some of the poetry she loved, some of which I can still recite today.

I gorged myself on her cooking — home-baked bread with the butter she and I churned; groundcherry pie; fried chicken from the flock Grandpa and I raised; and large sugar cookies kept in an earthen jar at the top of the steps to the cellar.

There was Sunday school and church on Sunday mornings and Christian Endeavor and church on Sunday evenings. I attended every church service except one, when Grandpa stayed home to convince me that I should believe in the virgin birth. He tried. I'll give him "A" for effort. But his grandson was rapidly becoming a heretic and it took more than his valiant efforts to change me.

During the day I often played in the sand pile Grandpa made for me, and I played the piano for hours on end. Occasionally I walked barefoot to Uncle Earl's farm. During the threshing season I sometimes lugged jugs of cold water to members of the threshing crew and then, at noon, ate with them. At other times I played with my younger cousins, Mabel and Catherine. In the evening or on Sundays we sometimes played croquet with the mallets made by Uncle Earl, Clarence and Paul from the hardwood on their farm.

The sandbox, the piano, and the trips to the farm were much more than fun. They were therapy for a lonely little lad trying to work out a new style of living without his

11

mother.

During the fourth summer with my grandparents, Grandma Kenworthy lovingly and cautiously introduced me to the idea of a stepmother. That was a difficult idea for me to accept, but little by little she won me over. I didn't know at the time that Dad was "seeing" Violet Cosand, although I did think he was spending an enormous amount of time helping her with the pageant she had written on "George Fox and The Quakers" and was getting ready to produce in the New London park.

Perhaps the foregoing paragraphs indicate what Margaret Mead meant in her autobiography, *Blackberry Winter*, when she wrote so convincingly about the important role grandparents can play in the lives of their grandchildren.

For several months after his return from the Soviet Union, Dad worked for the American Friends Service Committee, lecturing in many parts of the United States and raising money for its programs. During that period Wilmer and I were in Westtown School, a period in my life which is described in the next chapter.

Then Dad accepted an invitation to go to Washington, D.C., to work with Friends in the Irving Street Meeting, where he stayed for six years. Part of that time Dad and I lived together and I went to the nearby public schools. But much of my learning in Washington was from trips he and I took in that remarkable city. We visited the White House, the Capitol, the Smithsonian Institute, the Corcoran and Freer Art Galleries, and scores of other important and interesting places.

Since we had no service on Sunday evenings, Dad and I visited many churches and he told me simply and briefly about the different denominations they represented. One memorable Sunday morning we went to an early mass at a Catholic church in Baltimore, and later that morning Dad sat on the "facing benches" in the Quaker Meeting. That was a quiet lesson in interfaith understanding.

We also had one ticket to the lectures given by the National Geographic Society and took turns going to those wonderful events. When William Jennings Bryan came to Washington shortly before the Scopes trial, Dad took me to hear him. Dad was reading a book at the time by Fairfield Osborn on *The Earth Speaks to Bryan,* but he said that Bryan was a famous man and I should hear and see him.

Sometimes on Saturdays I played tennis on the public courts near the Washington Monument and Lincoln Memorial. On my way home one Saturday it was nearly an hour before I could get across Pennsylvania Avenue because there was a Ku Klux Klan parade of hooded marchers. Looking back on such an event gives one perspective on the enormous gains made in civil liberties and race relations since that time in the 1920s.

There were other memorable events such as the egg-rolling on the White House lawn at Easter time and the interdenominational Thanksgiving service in which Dad participated, and in which I sat directly behind President and Mrs. Coolidge in the section for V.I.P.'s.

One of the regular attenders at the Irving Street Meeting at that time was a Quaker woman from Kansas who worked with the Senate pages. She asked Dad if he would permit me to become a page, but he declined firmly. It was not until years later that I learned of that offer and I have often wondered what turn my life would have taken if he had said "Yes."

For a couple of years I attended the Powell Junior High School in Washington. The teaching was mediocre and I remember the name of only one instructor, Miss Melloy. I do recall my U.S. history teacher vaguely. She always wore black dresses, had a dirty face, and hated the Germans. That is all I can dredge up from a full year in her class. What a commentary on her teaching!

Miss Melloy was different. I studied civics with her and she encouraged me to visit the Senate and House on Saturdays. I suppose I got extra credit for those visits, but that didn't matter. I had a favorite doorman who used to point out the Senators who were speaking — such as Borah, Hiram Johnson, LaFollette and Norris.

Much of our life in Washington revolved around the Irving Street Meeting. It was a small group, drawn from a wide variety of Quaker groups in the United States. There were Friends in it from the Wilburite or conservative group, a few from the evangelical group, and several from the pastoral Meetings in the midwest and south.

That Meeting had never had a pastor and some members did not want one. But there were many differences among the various types of Quakers and after much soul-searching, they decided to ask Dad to become their pastor. He was selected largely because he understood the various groups and had a reputation as a conciliator.

At the Sunday morning service several Friends sat on the platform and they and other members of the Meeting spoke out of the silence. Dad always had a prepared message but he often spoke spontaneously on a theme which had developed early in the Meeting rather than using his prepared sermon. There was a piano on the side of the room and hymnals on the benches in case anyone asked for the group to sing. Such singing was frequent but not regular. This special type of service did not suit everyone, but it worked well for most members.

We also had a thriving Sunday school, and at the mid-week meetings Dad sometimes gave lectures such as a series of world religions which I still recall. We had fellowship suppers and picnics together and there was much visiting back and forth. Eventually that small group developed a fine sense of unity despite its differences.

Fortunately for me there was a sizeable group of boys my age. We were shepherded by Dr. Matthew Woodward, a medical doctor who worked for the government and was a Boy Scout leader. That group included Evan Brown, John Edgar Hiatt, Henry and Alfred Stanton, Joe Woodward, and others whose names I have forgotten. Sometimes we put on debates or some other type of program for the entire Meeting. Occasionally we took hikes together. And in the summer some of us played tennis near the home of the Stantons in Bethesda.

A similar group of young people included such persons

as Merrill Hiatt and Samuel Levering, both of whom have been prominent in Quaker circles since that time.

In the mid-1920s the Irving Street Meeting had a fire and part of their building was destroyed. At first it seemed like a disaster, but in some ways it was a blessing. At that time the I Street Meeting in Washington invited us to meet with them and out of that experience came several joint committees and eventually a plan for Dad to serve both groups as "secretary." In good Quaker fashion we were moving slowly toward union.

Then came the presidential election of 1928, with Herbert Hoover as the Republican candidate. He attended the I Street Meeting once or twice a year, but when he was attacked as a unitarian in theological beliefs, he started going to the Orthodox Meeting in Sandy Spring, Maryland, or to our Irving Street Meeting.

As head of the American and English Quaker work in the Soviet Union, Dad had known Hoover and was not one of his great admirers. Dad also knew that a minister in a church or Meeting attended by the President of the United States would not be free to speak frankly or even tangentially on social issues. Very reluctantly, therefore, Dad tendered his resignation.

In the next few months there was a concerted effort to force the two Quaker groups in Washington together. Soon a new Meeting was formed and a new building erected on Florida Avenue which President and Mrs. Hoover attended and to which they contributed generously. However, there were members in the I Street Meeting and in the Irving Street Meeting who either resented the way in which the union had been maneuvered or were opposed to any union. So for several years there were three Quaker groups in Washington. Today the Florida Avenue Meeting is a large and lively Meeting and has spawned three other groups. But it took years to heal the wounds caused by this precipitous action.

Meanwhile Dad had married Violet Cosand and we boys had acquired a mother (we never referred to her as our stepmother). She, too, had attended the New London high school and Earlham College, graduating in the same

15

class as Dad and Mamma. She had taught school for many years and had hundreds of devoted students. She was a quiet, sensitive, warm person with strong literary interests. In her quiet way she began to fill the void in Dad's life, to enrich the life of the Irving Street group, and to express her love for each of us boys. Of course it was difficult to be a stepmother, but she played that role magnificently until her death in 1970 at the age of 96.

CHAPTER 2

Westtown School,
Earlham College and Columbia University

With Mother's death, Dad was faced with many problems. One was what to do with three motherless boys. Of course, Carroll, the oldest, would continue at Earlham College. But what to do with Wilmer, 14, and Leonard, 10?

Because he would be working for at least a few months for the American Friends Service Committee and be based in Philadelphia, he enrolled Wilmer and me in Westtown School and found a room near the Westtown railroad station for himself. From there he could commute to and from Philadelphia and see us occasionally on Saturdays or Sundays.

Westtown is a boarding school for boys and girls located about 25 miles west of Philadelphia on 500 acres of rolling land in Chester County. Included on that large plot of land are a lake, a pine forest, orchards and a farm.

In the 1920s Westtown offered what was referred to as a "guarded education." Boys and girls were sent there to get a good Quaker education and that meant a classical college-preparatory program in a secluded environment. All the teachers were Friends and all the students were Friends or the children of Quakers. Each morning began with Bible reading at breakfast, and Meetings for Worship were held First Day and Fifth Day.

17

I was assigned to the Stone House where the younger boys lived. We were all too young to be away from home, but Westtown was probably the best place for most of us under circumstances like mine.

I was a lonely little lad in those days and the youngest boarding student in the school. Often in the afternoon I would get permission to take a walk, and spend my time playing in a nearby stream, building tiny dams and floating boats on the water. Occasionally I would go to the apartment of the house mother, Jesse Wood, to play her piano, or walk to the end of the lane where the Houghtons lived and play their piano. Those were the only pianos at Westtown as there were no music courses and no singing.

For the most part everything went well. But there were the inevitable troubles for such a young boarding student. For example, I recall vividly one occasion when the older boys asked me to do something which I refused to do. "I won't, I won't, I positively won't," I insisted. So the older boys formed a circle around me and took up the chant, "He won't. He won't. He positively won't." That went on until Jesse Wood heard the commotion and rescued me from my tormentors.

During my first year there I went to school in a downstairs room in the Stone House. The next year I was in a two-grade classroom in the main building under the care of Ruth Kellum. "Teacher Ruth," as she was called, had some difficulty with discipline, but she was remarkable in many ways. She took us on long hikes in the spring and we collected specimens of flowers. I collected and pressed over 100 varieties and mounted them in a book which I still cherish.

Teacher Ruth also devised an ingenious way of teaching geography. She gave each of us $1000, or some such amount, in imitation money and we planned a world trip, exchanging our American money for foreign currencies, writing accounts of the places we visited, and drawing illustrations of those places in our "logs." That was interdisciplinary learning of the first order.

In the fall we boys played soccer and in the winter

basketball — or we did workouts on the Swedish equipment which I hated. Two or three times a year school was dismissed early and students and faculty made an icy track for tobogganing. In the spring there was tennis, track or baseball.

I learned to skate at Westtown, to play soccer and tennis but I did not learn to swim. Something was wrong with an athletic program which did not teach everyone to swim when excellent facilities were available. It was not until years later that I learned to swim in the pool at Harvard.

Wilmer and I were awarded generous scholarships, so we worked as a partial repayment for those gifts. Albert Bailey was getting an arboretum started in those days and we worked many hours in it. In the fall we picked apples in the Westtown orchards. And in later years I helped to build The Greenwood, an outdoor ampitheater. For several years I also worked in the school library. Many of us worked and I do not recall feeling underprivileged because of such labor.

Some of my vacations were spent with the Russells in Swarthmore, Pennsylvania. And one memorable Christmas Wilmer and I spent with the Houghtons and their children — Willard, Daniel, Elwood, Fairchild and Florence.

Westtown was blessed in those days, as it is today, with several outstanding teachers, far more than one finds in most schools. The greatest debt I owe is to Carroll T. Brown. In the 1920s progressive education was coming into prominence and we knew that "Master Carroll" was vehemently opposed to it. Yet he was the very essence of a good progressive educator. For example, in our junior and senior years, he asked each student to pick an author or a topic and to read widely in that chosen field throughout the spring term. He helped each of us to select a field which was important to us. In my junior year I read the books of Hamlin Garland, such as *The Son of the Middle Border* and *The Daughter of the Middle Border,* thereby acquiring some roots in the middle west which I lacked because of the frequent moves of our family. Because of my keen interest in politics I read biographies of Lincoln and Wilson in my senior year. Each Monday we wrote essays on some phase of our reading during the past week. That gave us practice in writing essays and served to keep our reading up-to-date.

Master Carroll also served as the faculty adviser to *The Brown and White* (the student newspaper), and I spent many profitable hours with him in my capacity as editor. He was also the soccer coach, the skating instructor, and a frequent and welcome speaker in Meeting. He spent most of his life at Westtown and several generations of teachers were profoundly influenced by him.

There were other good teachers, too. Three of them were Elizabeth Page, Olive Charles and Caroline Nicholson.

Many of my subjects were easy for me. But I had difficulty with algebra and saw no sense to it. Latin was also tough for me, but several of us were helped by Tom Brown, a classmate, when we got up early in the mornings and sat in our bathrobes in an empty, cold classroom. And I doubt if I would have graduated, because of my ineptness in chemistry, except for the help of my roommate, Alfred Stanton, an old friend from Washington.

It is the richness of Westtown's extracurricular activities, however, which remain most vividly in my mind. Westtown still had elocution contests and I was able to make the finals in two such contests. Each year Westtown put on a Shakespeare play in The Greenwood and in my senior year I played the part of Shylock in *The Merchant of Venice*. I did not know any Jews and was able to play that role only by mimicking Albert Bailey, the coach. Perhaps this is an example of how we require students to study material too early or without sufficient experiential background.

My greatest learning experience was as editor of the student newspaper. With the help of Marianna Brown as assistant editor, Joe Conard as business manager, and a good staff, we turned out a first-rate paper. Especially helpful were the comments of my journalist brother,

Carroll, then in Japan. He wrote critiques of each issue, commending me especially for my editorials. I was especially proud of one which I thought at the time had brought about the introduction of music at Westtown. But I am sure now that that issue had been discussed many times by the faculty and by the School Committee before that revolutionary move was made.

Westtown was just beginning to inaugurate changes in those days which would alter its program significantly. Our class was the first to be allowed to put on a musical, "The Pirates of Penzance," but we were not permitted to wear costumes for it. And singing was introduced in the Sunday evening collection (a Westtown word for vespers), with Joe Holloway playing a tiny, portable organ while I led the singing.

Art, however, was much more respectable and Westtown prided itself on having a resident artist, George Gillette Whitney, an English Quaker and a close friend of N.C. Wyeth in nearby Chadds Ford. To my astonishment then, and even more today, I received one of the coveted Wyeth awards in art, largely for my sketch of one of the many squirrels on the campus.

George Whitney's wife, Janet Whitney, was another valued member of the Westtown community and she was just becoming famous as a novelist and biographer. Occasionally she invited a few of us to their home and read to us. She was also a frequent and acceptable speaker in our school Meeting for Worship.

There were no Negroes at Westtown in those days and some of us used to wonder what would happen if a Negro Quaker student applied. Within a few years, however, blacks were admitted to Westtown, beginning with the children of Ralph Bunche.

Westtown was a wonderful place, but some of us had stayed there too long. We knew the routines of the school intimately and were bored. To take out our frustrations, we resorted to some disrupting tactics. We nearly drove a lovely but incompetent French teacher crazy. We burned our notebooks from our Quakerism class in a protest bonfire on the soccer field. And on Alumni Day, replete with its Big Tent and hundreds of visitors, some members of the class collected the outdoor privies by the lake and placed them on floats.in that body of water, much to the chagrin of the school's administrators.

Nevertheless they put up with us that year and in June of 1929 graduated our class in the new and beautiful fieldstone Meeting House, with Rufus Jones, the most prominent Quaker in the United States, as the speaker. Five of us were commencement essayists — Rowland Bacon, Maryanna Palmer, Alfred Stanton, Helen Wright, and I. My essay was on "Yankee Imperialism in Latin America."

MY YEARS AT EARLHAM COLLEGE

Getting into colleges in those days was easy and I was admitted to Earlham without even considering the possibility that I might be turned down.

Our chief worry as students was financial. It was 1929 and the depression had just begun. We wondered whether our families could scrape together enough money to pay the tuition and board and room and still have some spending money. My earnings from the hotel work in the summers helped. So did a generous scholarship and the money I earned by selling shoes all day Saturday in the Hoosier Store. Nevertheless I knew that Dad and Mother were skimping and scraping to make my education possible, but I also knew that they were doing it willingly because they prized a college education for each of their sons.

In September 1929, I entered Earlham as a freshman. We had an orientation week which was relatively new then. From that period I recall very well President Dennis' remarks about "the golden mean" — the heart of his philosophy of life. And I remember his remarks about the importance of preparation for any task. He referred to the verb used in Washington — "to smoot" — which grew out of the fact that Senator Smoot was always prepared for committee meetings and speeches.

I also recall the goals which Dean Clyde Milner suggested to us for our college years. They were to

22

individualize, to socialize and to idealize.

Earlham at that time was a very good institution, even though it was not widely known. It had an excellent museum and was outstanding in the sciences. It was also outstanding in speech work. In fact, the first two departments of speech in American colleges were started by two brothers, Thomas Clarkson Trueblood and Edwin P. Trueblood, at the University of Michigan and at Earlham.

In 1929 Earlham also had a new president, William Cullen Dennis, an Earlham graduate who had had a distinguished career in international law. He was not an innovator in education, but an innovator was not needed at that point in Earlham's history. Survival was the most important goal and President Dennis was cautious, prudent and frugal, as well as wise. He kept the college going through the difficult days of the depression and he survived the furor that arose when dancing was introduced on the campus, an act which many midwestern Quakers considered as the recognition of Satan.

Because of his interest in world affairs, President Dennis developed an annual Institute of Polity, which brought several outstanding speakers to the campus for a week in the spring when all classes were cancelled and the students attended the lectures and forums.

President Dennis was also interested in hiking and in nature study. He developed a unique plan for an annual all-college outing in the fall to such places as Turkey Run and The Dunes, with several chapel programs on the locale to be visited.

When I entered Earlham, I was already known. I was the son of Murray and Violet Kenworthy or the brother of Carroll or Wilmer Kenworthy. That helped and hurt. It helped because I was a Kenworthy to many of the faculty and not just another freshman. It helped, too, because great expectations were placed in front of me. And it helped because several friends of my older brothers had younger brothers who were also freshmen, such as the Druleys, the Hamptons and the Johnsons. But it hurt because I was expected to be a football player and a track star, and I was not talented in either field. And it hurt because I was just another Kenworthy and not Leonard Kenworthy. But I survived and discovered that I could carve my own niche without trying to live up to the reputation of my family.

Those of us who had attended eastern prep schools found the academic work at Earlham relatively easy, especially in the first year. We were better prepared than the graduates of most midwestern high schools, except for those in places like Richmond and Indianapolis. At the end of the first semester there were several freshmen who had a straight "A" record and Dean Milner and his wife (who was also a dean) invited us to a waffle breakfast at their home. There he challenged us to maintain our excellent records and help Earlham to obtain a Phi Beta Kappa chapter. That did not happen in our years at Earlham, but it did happen later. Among those who were included in that group were David Dennis, Francis Hole, Malcolm Jolliff, Orville Johnson, Charles Wright and I — and possibly others.

During my Earlham years I had some outstanding teachers, although fewer than at Westtown. Probably the best professor I had was "Daddy" Hole. He was a graduate of Harvard and an eminent geologist who piled some of his students in an old truck every summer and took them on field trips to the west. He was excited about geology and communicated that excitement to us.

Evolution still bothered some people in the 1930s who saw it as a denial of the story of creation found in Genesis. Daddy Hole did not. He saw geology and evolution as confirmation of God's creative genius. To him, creation continued; God was still at work in nature and in human beings. He was a great teacher and a concerned Quaker, serving for a period as clerk of the Indiana Yearly Meeting of Friends.

Then there was E. Merrill Root, a poet and former student of Robert Frost. Root was writing poetry madly, gladly and voluminously in those days. He had recently published *East of Eden,* and other books were underway or churning in his mind. Often he would write three or four short poems on the blackboard and ask us to compare and contrast them. Eventually we realized that all of those poems were his handiwork. It was a new and exciting experience for us to study with a nationally famous writer.

In that period of his life he was a radical, politically. Imagine my surprise later in life to pick up a book in which Professor Root attacked most of the leaders of the social studies movement in the United States as communists or socialists. Apparently he had exchanged one orthodoxy — radicalism, for another — reactionaryism.

At Earlham the extracurricular or cocurricular activities meant at least as much to me as my courses. That was especially true of the a cappella choir. My membership in it was probably the greatest experience of my Earlham years. At that time the famous Westminster Choir was located in Dayton, Ohio, and its assistant director, Gustav Lehman, an Earlham graduate, came to Richmond each week to direct the Earlham College choir. We sang at the college, locally, and in nearby cities. During the spring vacation of my freshman year we made a grand tour of the east, singing to alumni groups, at several radio stations, and at the Chalfonte Haddon Hotel in Atlantic City, then in its heyday. From there we went on to Washington, D.C., where we gave a public concert and sang on the White House steps for the Hoover family and the White House staff.

We became a close-knit organization musically and personally and developed a deep affection for "Dad" Lehman. It was therefore a terrible blow to learn from him that he was leaving Dayton and Earlham for Colgate-Rochester Divinity School to train choir directors or ministers of music. Our final get-together was a memorable occasion. College students seldom cry when a professor leaves, but many of us did at that time.

In order to improve the quality of the singing in the choir and to give us individual help, Dad Lehman divided us into small groups. In them we sang solos. But he had a firm rule that there must be some favorable remark before

25

any negative comments were made, even if we had to compliment our colleagues on their dresses or ties. That was a valuable lesson and one I used later in my work with student teachers.

On a few occasions I played on the Earlham tennis team in matches with other colleges, but that was the extent of my intercollegiate athletics.

In public speaking, however, I was extremely active. I placed in seven oratorical contests and won the extempore speaking contest one year. Debating was still important at Earlham and making the debating team was an honor. For three years I was on the varsity, meeting with similar groups from several nearby colleges. One year one of the two varsity teams was composed entirely of members of the class of 1933. On it were David Dennis, Tom Millikan, and I, with Orville Johnson as the alternate. For practice we sometimes debated a team of college professors which included President Dennis, an international lawyer; Dean M.O. Ross, an economics professor; and Arthur Funston, a political science professor. Only in a small college is that likely to happen. As a result of these activities, I was elected to Tau Kappa Alpha, the national honorary forensic fraternity.

I was also deeply involved in journalism, first as managing editor of *The Earlham Post*, the college newspaper, and then as editor of *The Sargasso*, the college yearbook. Every four years Earlham has a lavish English May Day and 1933 was the year for that event. In our *Sargasso* we featured the historic roots of the college in England. The annual was dedicated to President Dennis; General John J. Pershing, Charles Evans Hughes of the Supreme Court, and Ambassador Hugh Gibson wrote testimonial letters about Dennis. It was certainly a distinctive book and the editor and staff received many laudatory comments.

The greatest honor I received in college, however, was the first prize in a North America Essay Contest sponsored by the Federal Council of Churches on the topic of "Christ and World Friendship." The check for $300 (a munificent sum in those days) was presented to me in the spring of 1931 at the annual Institute of Polity and the essay was printed in several religious publications. That money helped to tide me over a financially difficult period which lay ahead.

During those four years there were the usual parties, dates, dances, and escapades. Basketball loomed large in our lives, not only because we were in Indiana, but because we had a varsity team which won every game for over a year — quite a feat for a small Quaker college — and one which hastened the departure of the coach, Blair Gullion, to Cornell University.

I was fortunate in my roommates. In my freshman year I roomed with Forrest Hawkins. Another year I roomed with Tom Millikan. And for two years my roommate was Orville Johnson, who has served Earlham well in several capacities since that time, including several years as head of the Speech Department. Tom, Orville and I were also class presidents, with Orville serving twice in that capacity.

Those college years zoomed by and soon it was commencement time in 1933. In the last few weeks before that event, we talked much about jobs and vocations. I had considered four possibilities — journalism, the ministry, personnel work and teaching. In my senior year I was offered a small scholarship at the Medill School of Journalism at Northwestern University, but I decided to teach, with writing and speaking as sidelines. My major at Earlham had been history, but I had taken a minor in education and had done my student teaching in the Morton High School. So my preparation for that profession was well under way.

Because there were no jobs in teaching for me in 1933, I decided to go on to graduate school. At least I could get another degree and fill in the time profitably until more jobs were available. Little did I know then, however, how long that would be, with the depression extending for years. But it is sometimes good not to know how rough the road ahead is going to be.

SUMMER WORK IN THE POCONOS

In my sophomore year at Westtown I landed a summer

job in a small hotel which was an annex of The Inn at Pocono Manor. It was called The Oakwood and catered to Quakers who could not afford The Inn or who did not like its luxury. That job came largely as a result of the record my brother Wilmer had made there in previous summers. For the next seven summers I worked there full time, and when I was attending Harvard Summer School, I worked at The Oakwood for parts of the summer.

Many of the guests treated us as grandsons or nephews and were generous in their tips, so that we returned to school each fall with sizeable savings. The work there was such a good experience for some of the bellhops and waiters that they went on to the Cornell hotel school and into hotel work or related jobs as a lifetime vocation. Among them were Rowland Bacon, Harold Cope and Truman Wright.

WORKING ON MY M.A. AT COLUMBIA UNIVERSITY

When I thought about graduate work, I explored several possibilities but finally decided to go to Columbia, largely because of Carroll's interest and the fact that he had taken his M.A. there in international relations.

Fortunately I was able to get work in the offices of the men's dorms, mainly because of my work at The Oakwood. With that income, my summer's earnings, and the "nest egg" from the Van Loan Essay Contest, I was able to finance the year at Columbia.

During the first semester I took two courses in guidance at Teachers College, thinking I might go into high school counseling work. But all the other courses were in history at Columbia. In that department I soon learned that graduate work consisted largely of sitting, taking notes, reading, writing term papers and preparing a thesis.

David Muzzey was sometimes interesting as a speaker, especially when he told anecdotes about the famous and the near-famous in U.S. history, constantly winding and unwinding the ribbon of his pince-nez glasses as he talked. But most of the time he rambled.

Dixon Ryan Fox, attired on Saturday mornings in his grey pinstriped trousers and formal black coat, occasionally thrilled us with his lectures on early colonial leaders. We even applauded at the end of his lecture on George Washington, but he was not always so eloquent.

Allan Nevins, a former newspaperman who was already famous as an authority on the post-Civil War era and as a biographer of Grover Cleveland, peppered us with facts and sometimes challenged us with new interpretations of such maligned figures as Andrew Johnson and Samuel Tilden. But most of the time we did not rate him high as a lecturer.

Harry Carman was the only one who tried to elicit any discussion from his students. The response was only half-hearted because most graduates had come to hear him lecture, not to listen to the chatter of their classmates. How strange in retrospect to realize that I received the Harry J. Carman Award in the social sciences 40 years after sitting in his class at Columbia.

Most of my time and energy went into my thesis, which was a biography of Daniel Wolsey Voorhees, a Representative and Senator from Indiana for nearly 40 years, and a Democrat in the days when they were scarce in the north. Allan Nevins, my adviser, liked the idea because Voorhees had lived in the post-Civil War period and was a politician on whom no one had done research.

In the next few months I burrowed in the files of newspaper clippings in the School of Journalism Library at Columbia, turned hundreds of pages of decaying, brittle newspapers in the New York Public Library, scanned *The Congressional Record* for a period of several years, and consulted scores of books on the period in which Voorhees had lived.

Much of my writing was done as I sat at the switchboard in Livingston Hall, the graduate dorm in those days. So I was earning a little money as I wrote my thesis, something very few people have done. When the manuscript was completed, I took it to Professor Nevins and we talked for only the second time in my year under his tutelage. When he read the thesis, he was very

29

complimentary about the research and the writing and urged me to get it published. It appeared in 1936 from the presses of the Bruce Humphries publishing company in Boston with the title *The Tall Sycamore of the Wabash: Daniel Wolsey Voorhees,* illustrated with cartoons by the famous Tom Nast.

When the book appeared I sent a copy to Professor Nevins and he replied, in part, as follows:

> I have examined your *Voorhees* with care. It is excellent in every way. I feel pride in it. You are the third student in the past few years who has found a publisher and I think that is a remarkable feat.

At times during that year I had been low in spirits. I was working almost full time, taking a full graduate program and writing my thesis. It was too much, and my eyes tried to tell me that, but I was reluctant to listen. At times I thought I might give up my plans for teaching and go into hotel work or become a florist, jobs in which I would not be so dependent on my eyes. Fortunately Wilmer was working in Bayonne, New Jersey, during that period and his weekly visits helped me through that agonizing year.

Another milestone was passed. I was now Leonard Kenworthy, A.B., M.A. Now what?

CHAPTER 3

My Earliest Attempts at Teaching — and Harvard Summer School

The spring of 1934 passed slowly and at times tortuously at Columbia. The depression persisted and jobs were scarce or nonexistent. Despite my strenuous efforts, there wasn't a single job offer for the fall. In June I returned to Pocono Manor for another summer at The Oakwood. June went by. July passed. We were well into August and still there was no job in sight.

Toward the end of August, I received a letter from the president of Friends University in Wichita, Kansas. In it he offered me a job teaching speech. On paper the salary would be $2000, but I would be expected to waive half of that amount because of the financial difficulties of the college.

As I was mulling my reply, another letter arrived. It was from Walter Haviland, the headmaster of Friends Select School in Philadelphia. In it he asked if I would consider an "interneship" in that school. My room and board would be provided by friends of the school, Dr. Anna Sharpless and Dr. Helena Goodwin, in their home, and the school would give me $1 each day I worked. That would take care of my carfare and lunch.

I was not really interested in a job in speech or even in a college position and I felt that I was too liberal theologically to work comfortably with some Kansas

31

Friends. Working at Friends Select would not bring me much income, but it was a very good school and in a part of the country I knew and liked. And living in the home of Dr. Sharpless and Dr. Goodwin, two Quaker physicians, would be enriching in many ways.

Within a week my mind was made up and I wrote that I would like to come to Friends Select. So, early in September, I left the Poconos and went to live for a month in the home of Walter and Olive Haviland in Lansdowne until Dr. Sharpless and Dr. Goodwin returned to their winter home.

Living with the Havilands was a wonderful experience. Olive was editor of *The Friend*, one of two Quaker publications in Philadelphia at that time. After dinner each evening, Walter would read from a book of quotations from the religions of the world, arranged by topics. After a series of quotations, he would ask his wife from which religion the quotations came. Almost always she could tell.

Every morning I woke and heard Walter whistling, usually off-key, but enthusiastically, as he worked in his garden. Then came breakfast and a reckless ride to the center of Philadelphia where Friends Select was located. Walter was a fascinating guide but a mediocre driver. We careened around the corners while he pointed out places of historic interest, and every day I wondered if we would make it to the school alive.

During my first year at Friends Select, I did no regular teaching, but I substituted in several classes. I did have a dramatics club and struggled with it, for I was not adequately trained for such work. The students, however, were interested and overlooked my deficiencies — or didn't realize them. Most of the time I guided visitors around the school, ran the adding machine for the school bookkeeper, did research for Walter Haviland's talks and writing, and anything else which needed to be done.

Several of us were serving as internes in the various Quaker schools in the Philadelphia area that year and we formed an Internes Council which lasted for several years. I was elected president and Rachel Letchworth, secretary.

For the year 1935-36 I was invited to stay at Friends Select as assistant to the headmaster for the "magnificent" sum of $1200. I accepted gladly. That year I taught a seventh-grade course in geography and two sections of an eighth-grade science course — one for boys and one for girls. The geography course was fun and fairly easy to teach, but the science course was more difficult. Fortunately the Fels Planetarium was nearby and I took my classes there regularly for their programs. We did many experiments, several of which I tried out prior to class under the supervision of the high school science teacher. But the best learning experience for me came in the weekly science news programs we developed. Each student took his or her turn as the program director and arranged for different members of the class to report on articles from the *Science Newsletter*. We ran the programs as radio broadcasts and when I flicked the light, we were "on the air." It was gratifying that the students really thought of this as a live broadcast. Largely by chance, I learned the importance of such student involvement.

At one time during that second year Walter Haviland had to be away from the school for nearly a month and I was nominally in charge, even though I was the youngest member of the staff. That was indeed an experience. My real test as an acting headmaster came from a 9th grade girl who used her shiny pocketbook to catch the rays of the sun and reflect them all over the ceiling of the auditorium. I ignored her during the morning assembly, but at the close of the exercises, I grabbed her pocketbook and took it away from her. It was just about the worst thing I could have done. She was a disturbed adolescent, currently working with a psychiatrist, and all I did was challenge and provoke her. Her reaction was that of a tigress whose cub had been threatened. Only by calling on the school psychologist was I able to get out of that jam. However, that was my only real difficulty, thanks in large part to the help of a wise, tolerant and helpful staff.

When I had free time I visited the classes of some of the outstanding teachers. One was Mrs. Lowry, who was superb in working with gifted seniors in literature. Another was Ruth Goodwin, a graduate of Wellesley, and a scholar and a world traveler. Ruth had already introduced a course in Asian history in the 10th grade, something far ahead of current social studies practices. Since she lived with Dr. Sharpless and her sister, Dr. Goodwin, I had many opportunities to learn from her at home as well as at school.

Friends Select was ideally located for a city school — three blocks from City Hall in the heart of downtown Philadelphia, within a block of the suburban train station, and a couple of blocks from the subway. Parents who worked downtown could drive easily to and from the school, too. Furthermore it was within walking distance of the Commercial Museum, the Public Library, the Rodin Museum, the Philadelphia Art Museum, and the plant of the *Philadelphia Evening Bulletin*. Not too far away were Independence Hall and other historic spots. Unfortunately I made little progress in persuading the teachers to use this rich laboratory for learning.

Despite the fact that the school dated back to the days of William Penn and was the lineal descendant of several smaller Quaker schools, it had no endowment and little prospect of developing one. So its financial future was precarious. Alex Robinson, a math teacher and concerned Friend, and I dreamed up a plan to build a skyscraper on this valuable central city property and to rent the upper floors for additional income for the school. We submitted our plan to the School Committee which dismissed it as far-fetched. But nearly 30 years later, Friends Select adopted this idea and a skyscraper office building was built, with the school next door. Yes, 30 years later!

Walter Haviland seemed pleased with my work and told me that he hoped I would succeed him as headmaster, but not to mention it to anyone on the School Committee. And several members of the School Committee complimented me on my work and said they hoped I would eventually succeed Walter Haviland, but not to mention this to him.

However, I felt that I was much too young and inexperienced to become a headmaster and that a new and vigorous head of the school would not need an assistant. In addition, I was anxious to get into social studies teaching full time. So I kept searching for such a teaching position.

Such an opportunity came in 1936 from Thomas Burton of the Brunswick School in Greenwich, Connecticut. I took the train to New York City and on to Greenwich for an interview. With that trip I rode into a different world. Greenwich was one of the wealthiest suburbs in the United States and had four private schools. One of them was the Brunswick School, a small, college-preparatory institution for boys, with classes from kindergarten through the high school years.

Mr. Burton hired me and I moved to Greenwich in the fall. My salary was $2400, double what I had received at Friends Select the previous year. I was given five classes in the social studies, placed in charge of the Upper School assembly programs and the school library (manned by students), and given a playground assignment in the afternoon with some of the younger boys.

The headmaster gave me complete freedom with my classes and set up a room with tables so that I could conduct most classes in seminar style. He also gave me carte blanche in the selection of textbooks. Those I selected for the 7th and 8th grades were from the pioneering series of Harold Rugg of Teachers College, Columbia — a series which was later labeled "socialistic" by reactionary groups and eventually removed from most schools.

In two of the junior high school classes the boys worked on "contracts" and at their own pace. This was similar to the Dalton Plan, although I have no recollection of knowing about that approach. There was much merit in the individualization of that method, but the students lost the values which come from group discussion.

In the world history and United States history courses I hewed closely to college prep school styles of teaching as I did not feel ready to introduce anything more innovative at that time.

It was the ninth-grade course that really challenged me. It was supposed to be a community civics course, with emphasis upon the local community. I discovered a book on the history of Greenwich which we could use. But I didn't want to limit the course to that aspect of the social studies. So I created my own units. One was on propaganda and included a survey by students of the sales in Greenwich of magazines. Another was on public housing, a controversial issue at that time in U.S. life. As a part of that unit we visited the new housing project in nearby Stamford, taking parents with us as a safeguard against criticism of the trip. In the fall we studied the organizations in the Greenwich Community Chest, and the boys took an active part in that annual campaign. Later we studied the town budget and attended the representative town meeting where it was discussed. We were appalled by the tome which contained the annual report of our community and arranged with the Municipal League in New York City to set up a display in the Greenwich Public Library of simplified town reports from many other cities. As a result of that effort, Greenwich revised its annual report, inaugurating a short, readable, illustrated booklet — a type of publication which is still issued there.

This was a new type of teaching for a prep school and attracted considerable attention. *The Greenwich Press* commented favorably on it, urging the local schools to introduce such a course. At the suggestion of a colleague, whose wife was a Christian Scientist, I wrote an account of this course for the *Christian Science Monitor,* entitled "The Town as A Textbook." Eventually I spoke to the Middle States Council for the Social Studies on this course and its implications for other schools. And I was made co-chairman of the civic education committee of the National Council for the Social Studies.

Most of my students and parents were enthusiastic about these social studies courses, but I was never sure how far I could go in realistic teaching in a community with so many rich and often reactionary people. The

Board of Directors of the school held its monthly sessions around the tables in my classroom. One morning I entered the room and knew that they had met there the evening before because the room was saturated with cigar smoke. Then I spied one book in the center of the tables. It was Karl Marx's *Das Kapital.* The volume had been on the bookshelf in my classroom for use in the world history course, but we had not used it yet. Why it was on the table was never explained to me — and I never asked.

The Brunswick School was different from other schools I had known. For example, in one class of 11 boys, I had the sons of seven corporation presidents. I still remember my surprise to learn that the school had no basketball team. With a Hoosier background, that was inconceivable. But so was the idea of a varsity ice hockey team, three boat clubs, and a part-time instructor in sailing!

Living in Greenwich was a new and valuable experience for me. It was the home of many wealthy families such as the Rockefellers and the Gimbels. It was a community with a representative town meeting and an outstanding public library. And even though a school teacher was not really a part of the community, I was welcomed to many social occasions as a young bachelor. No one in Greenwich had ever heard of the Kenworthys and it was good for me at this point in my life to escape my family for a few years.

At the end of one school year I was asked to be the tutor in the Skakel home, taking care of their three boys while the parents were in Europe and coaching two of the boys for the College Boards in history. That was my introduction to life in the home of the nouveau riche, for Mr. Skakel was an extremely successful businessman who who had bought the sumptous estate of the Simmons family (of mattress fame). I thought I was to be merely the tutor of the three boys but it turned out that I was in charge of the entire household, including a cook, a chauffeur, a French-Swiss maid, a German refugee girl who cleaned the house, the grandmother, and the Skakel girls as well as the boys.

The first night I was there, Grandmother had a heart

attack and I had to summon a doctor in the middle of the night. Before the week was over the oldest boy had wrecked the family station wagon. Shortly after that I had to take a gun away from him lest he kill his younger brother. And there were other hair-raising escapades.

A cablegram arrived from Europe telling me to stay on after the July 4th date when I had intended to leave. I had expected to go to Harvard Summer School and was in no mood to spend the entire summer as head of such a household. So I cabled that I would carry out my commitment but not be available after the 4th. I still bear the scars on my neck from boils which I acquired as a result of my stay with the Skakels. And, of course, I have read with interest, and often with sympathy, news about that family over a period of many years as Ethel Skakel Kennedy and other members of that family have been in the newspapers frequently.

THREE SUMMERS OF STUDY AT HARVARD

That summer was the second of three wonderful summers at Harvard. During the first one I had taken a course in private school administration under the tutelage of Francis Spaulding, an eminent professor of education whose long and illustrious career included the chairmanship of the Study of the Character and Cost of Education in New York State and who was a pioneer in studies of the learning process.

Dr. Spaulding had been impressed with the case study method used by the Harvard Business School and was using that approach in his classes when I studied with him. Every two or three days he would present the group with a new problem in school administration and ask us to work out our solution to it. Today we call this inquiry or discovery learning; then it was known as the case study approach, and it was very effective.

At the beginning of the summer Dr. Spaulding asked each of us to list the two fields in which we felt most at home and the two in which we felt the most uncomfortable. A few days later he asked us to prepare term papers selected from one of our two weakest fields. I had listed science and math and in view of my work in science at Friends Select, I wrote on science teaching. The information I gained was invaluable and the method extraordinary.

The second summer at Harvard I worked with Dr. Howard E. Wilson. That was my first experience with the workshop approach in teacher education. Each of us worked on a problem which was real to him or her. Even though we worked individually and in small groups most of the time, we did have some large group experiences, including several trips in and around Boston. Occasionally we spent an evening in the home of Howard and Florence Wilson and those social times welded us together as a group. The workshop method was a tremendous experience for me and helped to reshape my philosophy of education and my teaching. Of course I had no idea at that time that Howard and I would be introducing that method years later to educators from many nations in UNESCO's first international workshop.

My third summer at Harvard was devoted to working on a textbook with Dr. Wilson. It was never published but some of the ideas were incorporated years later in a volume in my social studies series with Ginn and Company.

It was during my time at the Brunswick School and at Harvard that I was invited as one of 35 or so "promising social studies teachers" to spend two days with Charles Beard, the eminent historian. The occasion was the dedication of the new building for the Maxwell School of Citizenship at Syracuse University. Several of us literally sat at his feet for those two days. What a thrill for young social studies teachers in the 1930s.

CHAPTER 4

The Progressive Education Movement and the Eight Year Study at Friends Central School

In the 19th century two nations pioneered in providing education for all their children. They were Japan and the United States.

In our country the new public school system contributed significantly to our national well-being by providing all the children with the three R's, by helping to Americanize millions of immigrants, and by assisting future citizens to prepare for life in a democratic society.

But the introduction of mass education created enormous problems. Almost in desperation educators turned to the industrial system for a model. As a result, our schools were developed on the principle of mass production. Architects designed large boxes called schools. Inside those large boxes were smaller ones, called classrooms, and they were almost always the same shape and size. Then educators carved the curriculum into tiny boxes, called subjects. Furthermore, they divided the school day into boxes, called periods, with each period approximately the same size.

Inside those "factories" the teachers were the bosses and the students the workers. Of course there were incentives for the workers to produce, called grades and college credits.

The products of those factories were students steeped in the classics and ready to be shipped off to college for

41

further polishing. The rejects were shunted into vocational schools and eventually commanded lower prices on the open market.

SOME PROTESTS AGAINST MASS EDUCATION, AND SOME REFORMS

Of course there were critics of this type of mass education. For example, the Grange called for the inclusion of more practical subjects for future farmers and for the education of teachers specifically for rural schools. Many businessmen decried the emphasis upon the classics and urged the introduction of manual training and vocational education. And in the large cities some settlement house workers called for a type of education better suited to the needs of newcomers to the U.S.A. A few even championed the cause of cultural pluralism, helping immigrant children to retain the best of the Old World while gaining the best of the New.

The last decade of the 19th century and the first few years of the 20th were times of intellectual ferment in the United States, stimulated by the new ideas of Charles Darwin, the naturalist; Herbert Spencer, the philosopher; and others. Much of the new and creative thinking of that period was closely associated with education and with schools. There were many catalysts for change, but we shall mention only a few.

One was William James, who maintained that people should be active and creative agents in changing and improving their environment rather than merely keeping in tune with nature and adapting to the environment. He was eager to accentuate the values in individual differences, to develop well-trained and vigorous bodies as well as well-trained and vigorous minds, to find the moral equivalent of war, and to help build a better future for all people.

At about the same time G. Stanley Hall was establishing the first laboratories for the study of child growth and development, placing psychology on a scientific rather than a speculative basis. And Edward

Thorndike was trying to dissuade educators and others from the popular notion that human beings are essentially evil or basically good, asserting on the basis of his research that human nature is a mass of "original tendencies" which can be trained, depending upon one's purposes.

Around the turn of the century a progressive education movement developed comparable to the progressive movement in politics. Among the leaders then and in the next decades three stood out like Matterhorns, Kilimanjaros or Everests. They were Parker, Dewey and Kilpatrick.

Insufficient attention has been paid to Colonel Francis W. Parker, whom Dewey called "the father of progressive education." Shocked by the slaughter and suffering of the Civil War, he became convinced that people could learn to solve their differences without resorting to war and he envisioned schools as the training grounds for a new type of individual for a new type of society.

So he set out to improve the schools. As Jack Campbell points out in his superbly and sensitively written account of Parker, entitled *The Children's Crusader,* the keel was laid in Dayton for much of the new education which Parker was to launch for the whole nation. It was fashioned further in Quincy, Massachusetts, and then in Chicago.

Parker wanted to build schools which would resemble homes rather than dull, drab brick piles. In them education would be informal rather than formal. And in them children rather than subject matter would be the center. In place of learning about democracy in books, he wanted children to learn democracy in the classroom through participation in the making and enforcing of their own rules.

Rather than breaking down knowledge into compartments, he saw a natural unity to knowledge, like the universe itself. The subject matter of schools would be pivoted around students and would include scientific experiments, shop work for girls as well as boys, and art as central rather than peripheral. Methods would include motion pictures and field trips. And conferences with students and parents, and written comments, would replace grades.

At the heart of this new education would be a new type of teacher, conversant with society, with children, with learning, and with useful subject matter.

In his time Francis Parker achieved an outstanding record in implementing these and other innovative ideas.

Then there was John Dewey. Despite the efforts of his critics to disparage him and his ideas, he remains the most influential philosopher and educator in United States history. He played many roles, but he was primarily the philosopher of democracy and of the American experience. To him democracy was more than a form of government; it was "primarily a mode of associated living" or "a way of life controlled by a working faith in the possibilities of human nature."

He viewed children as children rather than as little adults, and he saw in them tremendous human potentialities when they were released by good homes and good schools in a vibrant society. Individualization or self-realization was central in his thinking, but he also stressed the creative relationship between individuals, pointing out that "shared experience is the greatest of human goods."

Experience or "learning by doing," as his idea has been expressed popularly, was the basis of growth. But he pointed out that knowledge needed to be buttressed and extended by imagination, since "Knowledge falters when imagination clips its wings or fears to use them."

Art was more important to him than to most philosophers and educators. "Art," he wrote, "celebrates with peculiar intensity the moments in which the past reenforces the present and in which the future is a quickening of what is now."

Dewey did not advocate permissive schools and complete freedom; he espoused first-rate schools with intellectual vigor, growing out of meaningful experiences, with students aided by first-rate teachers.

He had his limitations. He was a dreary lecturer, some

of his writings are difficult to understand, and he was not adept at putting his philosophy into practice in classrooms. But he was one of the "greats" in U.S. history and the most influential educator produced in our nation.

Fortunately for him and for the rest of us, William Heard Kilpatrick was a colleague of Dewey's at Columbia and was able to take Dewey's ideas and work out their implications for teaching. From Kilpatrick's thinking, experimentation and teaching emerged the activity-centered school, with its projects and units of study, organized around topics of interest to the learners. In such units most or all of the subject fields were used in a unified rather than a compartmentalized fashion. This was Deweyism in action in the classroom.

Kilpatrick had a powerful mind. He was a creative and prodigious worker. And he was a stimulating speaker and discussion leader. Thousands of teachers were thrilled by his classes at Teachers College, Columbia, and by his espousal of a new, functional, dynamic type of education. Back home they tried to put these ideas into practice in their classrooms.

In the early years of the progressive education movement in the U.S.A., its application was limited largely to independent schools and to a few demonstration schools connected with universities. But gradually progressive ideas were introduced into public school systems.

The public school system which pioneered the most in incorporating the ideas of progressive education into its program was the one in Winnetka, Illinois. When Carleton Washburne became superintendent of schools there in 1919, he began to organize small working teams of teachers who developed individualized programs in arithmetic and in reading. Later, similar work was done in art, music, science, the social studies, and other fields.

Typical of Washburne's emphasis upon experimentation based on solid research was a program which elicited the reactions of children in Winnetka, and in 500 cities across the United States, to the books they read. Their favorite books were then judged by librarians for their literary merit. Eventually Washburne wrote a summary of this research in a book called *The Right Book for the Right Child*. That was in the 1920s, long before individualized reading was known elsewhere.

Because of what they were doing and because of Washburne's skill in publicizing their efforts, Winnetka soon became the best-known school system in the world.

The Progressive Education Association Emerges

A progressive education movement had been underway for several years before a group of individuals founded the Progressive Education Association in 1919, with John Dewey as its honorary president.

In the early years of that association most of the members were from independent schools and most of them were concerned with elementary education. They did not agree on all aspects of the movement, but there was enough unity to hold them together. They believed in child-centered schools with an atmosphere of comparative freedom in which competition was minimized and cooperation maximized. So far as possible, their schools were democratic, with strenuous efforts made to develop in pupils self-discipline and to foster group decisions.

Those schools were pioneers in introducing health education, nature study, science and the social studies. Art, music and creative dramatics received far more attention than in most schools of that day. Subject matter borders were often obliterated as pupils worked on projects which required the use of several subjects. Individualization was fostered and testing minimized, except for some use of Thorndike's new tests.

Despite its tremendous influence upon American education, the membership of the P.E.A. remained small, reaching its peak with a little over 10,000 members.

As the years rolled by, more and more public schools became associated with that organization and the leadership for it came increasingly from professors in education departments in the middle west rather than from private school educators in the east.

THE EIGHT YEAR STUDY OR THE 30 SCHOOL EXPERIMENT

In 1934 the Progressive Education Association obtained funds from the Rockefeller General Education Board and from the Carnegie Corporation to launch the most extensive and comprehensive piece of research ever conducted in schools. It dealt with secondary education and was known as the Eight Year Study or the 30 School Experiment.

What that study proposed to do was to ascertain how well the students from secondary schools with progressive programs would do in colleges, including very traditional institutions. Many people assumed that the students from such schools would do poorly in colleges because they were not being educated for such institutions.

Thirty schools from various parts of the United States were invited to take part in the experiment. Some were private schools; others public.

Most of the colleges and universities were then asked if they would be willing to accept the graduates of the 30 schools upon the recommendations of the principals and teachers and with supporting evidence of the likelihood of their success in college. Almost all the colleges and universities agreed to this proposal. Consequently the schools were freed to carry on whatever type of programs they wanted to launch. Some became very innovative. Others tried out new ideas in some fields but not in others. A few were more timid, breaking little new ground.

THE EIGHT Year STUDY AT FRIENDS CENTRAL SCHOOL

In 1938 I was still at the Brunswick School in Greenwich, and happy in my work and in the community. Then came an inquiry from Barclay Jones, the headmaster of Friends Central School in Overbrook, Philadelphia, asking if I would come there to direct the social studies program of the school and teach classes in the upper two grades. I knew something about Friends Central because it was a Quaker school and a rival of

47

Friends Select. I had visited Friends Central since it had entered the Eight Year Study and had not been impressed with its work in the social studies.

Yet the idea intrigued me. Here was an opportunity to experiment with new ideas in the social studies and related fields. A move back to Philadelphia would also enable me to take an active part again in Quaker activities and to renew friendships with people in that area. So I visited the school again and was deeply impressed with Eleanor Stabler Clarke, the member of the Board who was most concerned with curriculum, and with Bob Cadigan, the head of the English Department, who was chiefly responsible for the school's part in the Eight Year Study.

Early in the fall of 1938 I moved back to Philadelphia, arriving in time to spend several days with Bob, the first of hundreds of hours of exciting collaboration with him over the next few years.

In an effort to be innovative, Friends Central had placed the social studies at the center of the curriculum in the last three years of high school. Students traced the history of the world from the beginning of recorded history to the present, in a three-year sequence. Most of the work in the English department dovetailed with the work in history. This was a different approach, but it did not appeal to me. Consequently I was encouraged to develop my own ideas for those three years.

In the 10th grade an abbreviated world history course was instituted with increased emphasis upon modern times. Some correlation was continued with the English and art departments, but less than in the previous four years because I felt that those subjects had become handmaidens to the social studies.

In the junior year United States history was reinstated but instead of offering a repetition of previous courses, based on a strictly chronological basis, I developed a series of units on topics starting with the present and then going back into history to trace the development of those ideas. The units we developed were:

Our Land — the U.S.A.

We the People of the United States: Today and

Yesterday

Farms and Factories: The Industrialization of the U.S.A.

Democracy and Its Development

Isolationism versus Internationalism

Great Men and Women Who Helped To Make the U.S.A.

Actually most of those units concentrated on one of the social science disciplines, thus anticipating by about 25 years the multidisciplinary approach to the social studies. In order to see each theme in relation to the others, I developed a large chart of U.S. history, showing these various strands in each period of our development as a nation. This was hung in a prominent place in the classroom and frequently used. Then, at the end of the year, we reviewed U.S. history in a more traditional manner.

Bernice Woerner was in charge of the literature work for the junior class and we decided we would correlate our work at times but go our separate way at many points. In that way we preserved the integrity of the English work. However, there were times when we worked together closely. That was especially true when we were working on the units on "We the People" and on "Great Men and Women Who Helped To Make the U.S.A." Both those units lent themselves admirably to the use of literature.

Occasionally we put our classes together for double periods with illustrated talks on American Art by Hobson Pittman or for group singing and the use of records of American Music under the leadership of Helen Kirk Schmidt.

The students visited the Philadelphia Art Museum several times and all of us saw plays together, such as *Abe Lincoln in Illinois*, starring Raymond Massey. In addition, we used the superb series of recordings on "Americans All — Immigrants All," produced by Rachel Davis DuBois for the U.S. Office of Education.

In reality that was an American Studies course, long before other schools used such an approach. The students reported on anonymous evaluation sheets that they enjoyed most the unit on "We the People," but learned the most in the unit on "Farms and Factories," primarily an economics unit.

If I were to teach that course today, I would drop the unit on "Great Men and Women" and incorporate that material in other units. In its place I would substitute a unit on "The Cultural Development of the United States." Otherwise I would offer the course in much the same way that I did many years ago.

It was in the senior year that we were most creative. That class consisted of approximately 70 students and we divided them into three sections of a course called "The Individual and Society," which Bob Cadigan, Molly Crookston and I taught, in what would be called today "team teaching."

In order to provide longer periods for uninterrupted concentration on a topic, each of us met with a group of students for 1½ hours a day for a period of five weeks. Our sections met simultaneously and in the afternoons. In that way classes could take trips or meet together occasionally for films, panels or lectures by invited guests.

With Bob Cadigan, the students explored literature which focused on the role of individuals in U.S. society and in other cultures. Bob had done his honors work at Swarthmore College in social drama and he made very effective use of that rich background at Friends Central. Some creative writing was also carried on, unrelated to the work of the combined classes.

Molly Crookston was the director of the nursery school in the morning and in the afternoon she guided the seniors in their study of psychology, making much use of Harry Overstreet's popular book *About Ourselves*. In addition there was some sex education, using Alice Keliher's *Life and Growth*. Trips were an essential part of the work with Molly, including visits to such places as the Overbrook School for the Blind and the Byeberry Mental Hospital.

At the time we were developing this Senior Enterprise Course, there was interest on the part of many students in communism in the U.S.S.R. and in fascism in Germany and Italy. Some seniors were also interested in attempts in the U.S.A. to pull ourselves out of the depression. So in the social studies segments of the senior course we tried to capitalize upon those interests. Two units were developed — Contemporary Problems in Other Lands and Contemporary Problems in the U.S.A.

We started with the unit on problems abroad because students had just had a year of United States history and because their study of how the U.S.S.R., Italy or Germany, and the Scandinavian countries had tried to meet their problems was good background for the study of contemporary problems in the U.S.A. In Cadigan's section these students read the literature of those same cultural areas.

Occasionally we brought the three sections together to view the excerpts from contemporary movies which the Commission on Human Relations of the Progressive Education Association had developed. We did not have tape recorders in those days, but we did make stenographic records of the discussions of the films and they were analyzed by experts in the Eight Year Study for evidences of critical thinking and changes in attitudes.

In order to tie the three segments of this total course together, we asked students to keep notebooks on the 10 major aspects of living in any society, drawing material from the minicourses of Cadigan, Crookston and Kenworthy. At the end of the year we asked students to prepare a paper which summarized and synthesized what they had learned about individuals as members of a family, community, nation and the international community. Some prepared radio scripts. A few made summaries in newspaper form. Others wrote papers. One student, Paul Griffith, wrote a biography of Thomas Mann as a member of his family, nation and the world. That essay was so good that it was read at commencement.

A unique feature of our work one year was a series of 15 radio programs on Saturday mornings over station W.I.P. which we and the students carried on as unrehearsed discussions based on an opening skit which

Bob usually wrote.

One year I took four boys to Washington for a four-day conference. I have lost track of two of them, but one was Dan Redmond, who has long been the editor of *Current History*, and another was Jep Carrell, who was a city manager in several communities and is now the president of a consortium of colleges in Ohio.

There were other parts of the curriculum which were affected by the Eight Year Study. One was a general science course taught by Eleanor Jones and Clayton Farraday; another was a very realistic health education course taught by Eliza Blackburn. Art was given special prominence, too. But it was the English and social studies work which was at the heart of our program.

The Help of Curriculum Specialists

Much of our motivation for experimentation came from stimulating contacts with other teachers and with curriculum specialists at conferences on the Eight Year Study. Even more help came from the visits of the curriculum specialists of the Eight Year Study staff.

One of those specialists was Hilda Taba. With her I.B.M. mind, her keen interest in social problems, and her ability to evaluate the results of teaching by ingenious tests, she challenged my thinking enormously. One day, for example, she asked me why I was spending so much time and energy teaching about war and peace. With a bit of a chip on my shoulder, I began to defend myself. She interrupted me to say that she agreed on the importance of such work but the test scores revealed that our students were already at the top in their attitudes in this area, compared with students in the 29 other schools.

Then she inquired what I was teaching about housing. When I replied, "Nothing," she showed me evidence that our students were at the bottom of the heap in that respect. So I visited Greenbelt in Maryland, Radburn in New Jersey, and several housing projects in New York City, taking pictures to use as slides in a unit I devised on housing. Soon the Taba tests showed tremendous changes in the attitudes of our students on this issue.

52

Sam McCutchen was another stimulating specialist who visited us from time to time. One day when he was visiting my class, I was teaching about Andrew Jackson. I was excited about the subject and thought the discussion went well. But Sam asked me after class why I thought Jackson was so important. Then I launched into a short lecture on the importance of teaching about democracy. "Fine," he said, cutting me short, "but do you have to discuss Jackson to develop that important idea?" His questioning then and at other times sparked a recasting of much of my teaching so that I was constantly examining with students "big ideas" or "concepts."

Another important facet of our work was demonstration teaching. Scores of teachers visited our classes and I suspect I taught better because they were there.

Several times I was asked to speak to social studies groups, and I wrote two articles on our work at Friends Central. One was on "Developing Social Sensitivity," and was published in *Secondary Education*. The other was on "Better Citizens for a Better World," which appeared in *Educational Outlook*.

A new dimension was added to my teaching by an invitation to join a small group of young people in Philadelphia who were interested in civic reform. That group was called the City Policy Committee and was patterned after the older group known as The Committee of Seventy. It was members of that City Policy Committee who sparked the reform movement in city government in Philadelphia in the 50s and 60s. But by that time I had left Philadelphia and was therefore not a part of that revolution.

Evaluating the Results of the Eight Year Study

Perhaps you as a reader have been wondering what happened to our students when they went on to college. To test their record there, each student from the 30 schools was matched with a counterpart or a control, without either person knowing who the other was. Great care was exercised in the selection of the counterparts so that the two persons were as nearly "identical twins" as possible in such factors as home background, I.Q. and high school scholastic record.

The results were clear. In their college courses the students from the progressive schools did at least as well as their controls from the more traditional schools, and in many cases, better, based on their grades. Only in mathematics and in formal grammar did the 30 school students fall behind their "twins." Judged by other criteria, the students from the 30 schools did far better than their counterparts. They showed more intellectual curiosity, more objectivity in their thinking and more appreciation of the arts. They received more academic honors, held a larger proportion of offices in campus organizations, and demonstrated more concern for people in the United States and around the globe. These comments were made by their professors and other key persons in the various colleges. And the professors were not likely to grant any special favors to the students from the 30 schools. In fact, many of the professors had been critical of the experiment at first, thinking that their colleges would be deluged with poorly prepared students. Even more arresting was the fact that the students who were rated highest came from the schools which had changed their curricula most radically.

This study was a landmark in American secondary and college education. Yet much of its potential impact has been lost and it is usually accorded only a few lines or a footnote in books on American education.

THE DEATH OF THE PROGRESSIVE EDUCATION ASSOCIATION

The failure of the Eight Year Study to create greater waves is explained by the history of the United States in the 30s, 40s, and 50s, and by the history of the Progressive Education Association.

As a result of the depression, several educators began to wrestle with the role of schools in our society. Many of the leaders in that movement were professors at Teachers College, Columbia — John Childs, George Counts, William Heard Kilpatrick, Harold Rugg, Goodwin Watson, and to some extent John Dewey. They studied American society and debated the role of schools in times like the ones in which they were living. Their views differed, but they were all convinced that schools should be more responsive to society than they had been and that students should be sent into society with a clearer understanding of it and an ability to live in it intelligently, as well as being able to help to transform it.

Space precludes a long account of their efforts, but two events should suffice to show the temper of the times and the thinking of those educational pioneers. In 1932 George Counts shook the Progressive Education Association with an address on "Dare Progressive Education Be Progressive?" published later as a small book entitled *Dare the Schools Build a New Social Order?* The subsequent discussion of the philosophy behind that statement split the Progressive Education Association and eventually torpedoed it. Many of the child-centered school advocates were shocked and dismayed. Many teachers were frightened lest they be characterized back home as radicals, socialists or even communists.

There seemed to be no middle ground, such as educating the planners of a new society without trying to actually plan a new society. The Association might have weathered the storm, too, if it had not tried to write a statement of its philosophy, for the writing of creeds almost always causes splits. The lines were drawn and no one seemed willing to budge an inch. A long, bitter and sometimes personal struggle ensued. Eventually the social reconstructionists won, but in the process the Progressive Education Association was destroyed. Efforts have been made in recent years to revive it but so far without much success.

There were other reasons for the death of the P.E.A. In his highly readable volume on *The Transformation of the Schools*, Lawrence Cremin mentions seven of them. One was the creation of factions. A second was the

negativism of all social reform movements — the fact that
the leaders know what they are against but not always
what they are for. A third explanation lay in the
inordinate demands this new type of education made on
classroom teachers. Fourth is the fact that the P.E.A.
was a victim of its own success — holding to stated
positions rather than constantly renewing itself. Fifth
was the definite swing in the U.S.A. in the 1940 s to a
much more conservative point of view, characterized by
McCarthyism. Cremin suggests that the movement relied
too heavily upon professional educators, rather than
broadening itself to include lay people. And seventh, the
movement and the Association collapsed because it failed
to keep pace with the continuing transformation of American society.

I would add two others. One was the fact that most of
the leaders of that movement and of the Association were
strong individualists and some of them prima donnas, a
point which might be a part of Cremin's first contention.
The other is that people were caught up in the war effort
in the 40s and educational experimentation was one of the
casualties of World War II.

In 1955 the Progressive Education Association was
officially and legally disbanded. It had served many
useful purposes in its short life and it was tragic that it
was abandoned. But the encouraging fact is that many of
the ideas of that movement have become a part of the
educational philosophy of thousands of teachers and that
many of the innovations it brought about have been
incorporated in school systems. Furthermore a new
movement for educational innovation appeared in the
1960s and is still with us in the 70s. Whereas many of the
changes in the 1920s and 1930s were carried out on the
basis of hunches or intuition, today's changes are being
based upon scientific research and experimentation. And
in the case of "the open classroom" movement, there is
now the halo of British respectability to give it credence in
the eyes of many Americans.

CHAPTER 5

Working for the American Friends Service Committee in Nazi Germany

Late in the spring of 1940 I was handed a note at the close of school asking me to call Clarence Pickett. He was a friend of the family, having taught both of my brothers at Earlham and having served with Dad and Tom Kelly on the steering committee of the American Friends Service Committee in Richmond. Now he was executive secretary of the A.F.S.C. in Philadelphia, and I often saw him and his wife, Lilly, at the Providence Road Meeting where we were all members. But why was he calling me?

The mystery was solved the following Saturday when I drove to the Pickett home in Wallingford. There he told me that the Service Committee was looking for someone to become director of the Friends International Center in Berlin. The job was primarily one of assisting people in leaving Germany. At that time Jewish refugees were being taken care of by a Jewish organization. Former Jews who were now Catholics were being taken care of by a Catholic group and those Jews who had become Lutherans were being taken care of by the Gruber Buro. But there were many people of Jewish ancestry who were without any religious affiliation and the Quakers were attempting to help them.

Clarence said that the Service Committee had considered several persons and hoped I would be willing to accept this assignment. The suggestion was breath taking. In some ways it seemed foolhardy to go to

57

Germany at such a time, but the invitation also appealed to me. Here was a rare opportunity to live in a nation at war and to have a front-row seat for an important event in world history. Furthermore, there was the appeal of Quaker and family tradition to serve in a difficult situation.

I was convinced that there were many people in Germany who believed in democracy, in everyday Christianity, and in tolerance and understanding of all religious groups. Such people were in trouble, and if my presence there as a representative of men and women of good will would help, then I should go. It might be foolhardy, but sometimes it is important to be one of "God's fools," as Kagawa once described such people. I was also encouraged by the fact that Henry Cadbury, an eminent biblical scholar at Harvard and a wise and esteemed Friend, would be there as an elder statesman.

I arranged for a leave of absence from Friends Central and set off in June of 1940 for Europe, flying first to Portugal. I was forced to stay in Lisbon for several days before getting a plane seat to Rome. There I experienced my first blackout, and was introduced to work with refugees by Howard Comfort, the director of the Friends International Center. During the day I served an apprenticeship with him. Then, in our spare time, he showed me Rome.

Reaching Berlin in July, I learned that Howard Elkinton and Alice Shaffer would have to leave Berlin within a week and that Henry Cadbury would be unable to come to Germany. In addition, local Quakers thought it would be best for me to live in a hotel rather than to stay with a German family.

Fortunately there was a small but competent staff in the Friends International Center — Frau Wedemeyer, Eva Schaal and Dorothe Kaske. With their help I immediately plunged into the job of interviewing people who wanted help to emigrate. Some needed affidavits or guarantees of support from people in the U.S.A. Others needed advice. Many needed the ear of a person in whom they could confide. Hounded by officials and haunted by real or imaginary fears, they needed friendliness and kindness most of all.

A few persons could be helped to emigrate to Shanghai, the Virgin Islands, parts of South America, or the United States. Those who stayed behind needed assistance in making life a little more bearable in Nazi Germany.

There were conferences with the representatives of the other refugee agencies — memorable hours with some of the finest religious leaders in Germany, made even more memorable by the fact that two of the men with whom I conferred were interned in concentration camps before I left Germany. There were contacts, too, with a Lutheran minister, Pfarrer Pilchau, who was in charge of counseling the families of conscientious objectors — most of them Jehovah's Witnesses. For a while I saw him often. Then he suggested that it would be wise for us not to see each other.

In various parts of Germany there were tiny Quaker groups, and when it became clear that Henry Cadbury was not coming, German Friends asked me to undertake occasional visits to those groups. But what could an American Friend, coming from a land of affluence and of comparative political calm, say to German Quakers and seekers? Naturally I realized that one cannot help others unless he has helped himself, or deepen the spiritual lives of others unless he has already begun to deepen his own spiritual life. Consequently I began an intensive search for spiritual strength. I read widely, including the journals of George Fox and John Woolman, and I read Harry Emerson Fosdick's *Meaning of Prayer* and *Meaning of Service*. I reread Paul's letters to the new churches and found many parallels with the contemporary scene in Germany. Music became an ever greater source of renewal for me and prayer took on increased significance.

Tom Kelly, raised later by Friends almost to sainthood, had been in Germany in 1938 and had traveled widely among Quakers there. His life had been transformed by that experience. In January of 1941 he wrote me, saying, "I can well imagine how rich your experience is, enriching both because of novel experiences and because of inward depths which are opened through suffering with others. May you grow to the full measure life there calls forth." That letter, written a week before he died, arrived at the end of February. Its receipt under those circumstances was a tremendously moving experience.

My religious experience was not as striking as Tom Kelly's had been, but something was happening. I knew it and others seemed to sense it. In a letter to my father, after a brief visit Douglas Steere made to Germany, he said, "the work in Berlin is maturing his spiritual life in a unique and wonderful way."

Soon I began to work on several talks for my visits with Friends. One was about "George Fox — Seeker." Another was about "Contagious Christians — Contagious Quakers," a title which caused consternation on the part of the Friend who translated it into German for me, as the word "contagious" in German refers almost exclusively to disease, laughter or yawning.

As I became acquainted with several remarkable people and they shared with me the intimate details of their spiritual journeys, I wrote on "Sources of Power for Times Like These," drawing upon their experiences without mentioning their names. More than other messages, that one seemed to speak to the condition of most of the seekers I met.

Later all three of those talks were printed in *Der Quaeker* and eventually appeared in my book *Toward A Fourth Century of Quakerism*.

During my year in Germany I was able to meet nearly all of the 275 members of the Society of Friends. That is a very small number of people but many of them were extraordinary individuals. In Nazi Germany one did not join such a group or retain membership in it lightly.

Most of the trips went well, but there were a few harrowing experiences. One was on a visit to Chemnitz for a Quarterly Meeting there. I registered in a small hotel and retired early. Around five in the morning I awoke to find two men standing at the foot of my bed. "Wir sind von der Geheimpolizei (the Gestapo)," they told me. Despite the hour and the shock to find them there, I was able to ask them what they wanted. They replied that they wanted to know what I was doing in Chemnitz. I said that I was a representative of the Quaker movement and was there to give a speech. "Ah, ja," one of them responded, saying that he knew about the Quaker Oats Company because his children ate those oats every morning. How does one correct that slight misconception of Quakers to the secret police at five o'clock in the morning? I tried, referring to the Quaker feeding in Germany after World War I. That helped. Soon they left, and what was more important, I stayed in the hotel room. Later I learned that the Minister of Foreign Affairs of Japan was passing through Chemnitz that day and the police were checking on all foreigners in that city and in other towns along his route.

It was with the Berlin Quaker group, however, that I was most active. I attended services with them almost every Sunday. The attendance ranged from 25 to 50 and the meetings were often moving. Sometimes the boots of soldiers, marching in the courtyard outside, disturbed the silence. But those boots also reminded us of our need for other kinds of strength to survive in such times.

Occasionally I spoke in Meeting, briefly, and in English. But when my remarks of three or four minutes took 10 to 15 minutes in translation, I knew that there was much of Emil Fuch's thoughts in the translation! When Friends asked me to consider speaking in German, I did so, thus saving us many minutes for silence.

I also took part in the monthly business sessions of the Berlin Quakers and in some of the activities of the Young Friends group, the only one of its kind in Germany. Almost every week I worked with the local Quakers as they packed books, musical instruments, and games for distribution by the International Y.M.C.A. in the stalags or prisoner-of-war camps for English and French soldiers incarcerated in Germany. Yes, that was possible in Hitler Germany — and what courage it took to carry on such work.

Once a month there was a public lecture at the International Center. I attended all of those lectures and even gave a couple myself.

Berlin Friends were most hospitable and I spent many Saturdays and Sundays with them in their homes. Often I spent a day with Lotte and Franz Hoffman and their daughter Isi in the suburbs. Lotte was a musician and Franz an architect of the famous Bauhaus group, who had lost his job when Hitler came to power. Occasionally I visited Clara Schwanke, a children's worker who had turned her home into a refuge for children, including some whose parents were in concentration camps. I played with the children, sang with them, and even washed dishes with them. When I left Germany, they presented me with a book of drawings. Prominent in it were drawings of "Onkel Leonhard" drying dishes, something rare in Germany in those days for a man.

Then there was the Vienna office. It was larger than our Berlin Center and in the year I was in Germany, they were able to help 500 or so people emigrate, whereas our Berlin office was able to help only 150 or so.

In February of 1941 I received a phone call from Frau Neumeyer, the director of the Vienna bureau. It was a brief, hurried, cryptic message, but I understood it and the urgency as well as the courage of that call. "They are being put onto trains, a thousand a train. Two trains have left. We are doing what we can. Can you come?" That was all she said. But I knew that "they" referred to the Jews and that they were being sent to Poland and eventually to extermination camps. I grabbed my bag and made the next train to Vienna.

The next few days were grim — the worst of my life. Scores of people crowded into our office, hoping somehow that we could help. Immediately I called Joe Roland, a graduate of the Germantown Friends School who worked in the U.S. consulate. He was able to give me a list of persons whose emigration papers were far enough along to warrant special attention. Then I met with groups of 20 to 25 persons and told them that we would help in every way possible even though I could not see each of them individually. But I did meet with those I thought we could help most.

Meanwhile Greta Sumpf, a German Quaker in the Vienna office, had organized a small group of people to collect blankets, thermos bottles, and whatever food they could assemble. Those items were brought to our office and given to the people who had been called up for the trains to Poland. She also planned a series of religious services for those who wanted to attend, and many did. Those services were simple, with some music, some poetry, and carefully chosen passages from the Old Testament. Those meetings were conducted with great compassion by Greta.

But the trains kept rolling and we were powerless to stop them. At the station were many friends of those who had been herded onto the trains. With them they brought small packages, symbols of their affection. Even being present at such a time was a testimony of their friendship.

At times I recalled George Arliss in the film, *The Man Who Played God*, for there were choices to be made and I was the only one who could make them. I also recalled Dad's comment that he had saved the lives of children in the Soviet Union and had consequently saved a generation of orphans. So when I had choices to make, I tried to help families rather than individuals.

There was a blind man who pushed his way into my office, despite the fact that he had no chance to emigrate. With bitterness he told me that I was not saving his life because he was blind. What does one say to a man at such a time? All I could say was that I was doing the best I could in a tragic situation completely beyond my control. From time to time, however, the memory of his face and his forefinger jabbed into my face, still haunt me.

Within a few days the trains stopped as suddenly as they had begun. No one knew why. Perhaps because they were needed more desperately to transport troops or materiel.

LEARNING ABOUT LIFE IN GERMANY

One of my purposes in going to Germany was to try to understand what had happened in that land of highly educated people, and to see if I could learn some lessons from that experience to share with others. Fortunately Hans Albrecht, the clerk of the German Yearly Meeting and the chairman of the Berlin International Center Committee, encouraged me to learn about German history and the contemporary scene.

One of the most vivid experiences of my life took place during my first week in Berlin. It was the Narvik victory parade on Unter den Linden. I am certain that some of the Berlin Quakers were displeased to know that I planned to see that parade, but I tried to explain why I wanted to do so. I went alone, trying to keep on the edges of the crowd. But I was soon pushed into the maelstrom. When the crowd took the Hitler salute and I didn't, I expected trouble. But nothing happened. Later I surmised that my glasses, my hat and my clothes identified me as a foreigner. Or the fact that I did not take the Hitler salute — which I never did in an entire year in Germany.

At that parade I was impressed with the use of flags, of music, of the mass salute, and the speeches, all calculated to stir the emotions of thousands of people. Then and later I wondered why these tools could be used for such diabolical purposes and not for worthy ones. This idea stayed with me and I kept wondering how the emotions of people, as well as their minds, could be channeled for worthwhile goals.

Erik Erikson might use this event to explain my belated "identity crisis," for it had a profound effect on me, propelling me into a lifetime of education for peace and social justice.

As I studied German history and the contemporary scene, it seemed to me that one of the major difficulties in Germany lay in the apathy of so many people. I estimated that a small segment of the people were ardent Nazis and that a still smaller group were openly opposed to that regime. The rest were apathetic or unwilling to go against the Nazi tide. At times I have felt the same about people in the United States, especially in the McCarthy era.

On various trips I tried to see some of the historic spots of German history. In Weimar I saw the hall where the

Weimar Republic was formed, and the statue to Goethe and Schiller, two of Germany's contributors to world culture. In Eisenach I visited Die Wartburg, the castle where Luther translated the New Testament into German so that the common people could have access to it. Later, Emil Fuchs, a renowned biblical scholar and an outstanding German Quaker, compared Martin Luther and George Fox for me. Emil felt that the young Luther was a tremendous person, but that he compromised with officialdom early in his career and lost his vision of Christianity. Emil felt that Fox had taken up where Luther left off and had maintained his vision throughout his life. Therefore Emil accorded Fox the role of The Great Reformer. It was a fascinating and new interpretation for me.

One of the startling impressions to a newcomer in Nazi Germany was the fact that life continued so normally for so many persons, despite the war. In Berlin, for example, four of Shakespeare's plays were being produced at one time in 1940-1941. The opera and church music seemed to draw even larger crowds than in normal times, although the concerts in the churches were musical performances for most people, rather than religious experiences.

But there were plenty of signs of the war, too. One was the air raids. They were few at first but became more frequent and more frightening or even more welcome to me? I kept a little bag packed and ready to grab when the siren sounded. Our hotel air raid shelter was relatively comfortable and I sometimes dozed there. Occasionally, however, I slept through an air raid. I would hear the siren and go to the basement, only to discover that what I had heard was the "all free" signal.

From time to time I was visited in the office by some member of the Gestapo. Usually they were perfunctory visits, but in April 1941, I received a phone call from the secret police which was different. I invited them to the office, but they insisted that I come to their headquarters. Soon I became aware that this was not the usual type of call and I asked what they had in mind, discovering that they were interested in the activities of the Berlin Quaker group. That meant that I had to think fast since I was in no way responsible for their activities. Nevertheless I did not want to involve local Friends if I could avoid it. We talked and I decided that the work of the International Center and my stay in Germany were at stake. So I told the official I was not responsible for the Berlin Quaker group and was granted permission to bring someone from that group with me.

I called Olga Halle, the clerk of the Meeting, who agreed to go. Once there, I sensed that the police wanted to make a case against me as a fifth columnist. They accused me of being the preacher and of preaching against the government. I replied that we did not have a preacher and that we did not discuss the government in our services. Apparently the officer thought I was lying. "How can you have a church and no preacher?" he asked. I tried to explain. It is difficult enough to describe a Quaker service on the basis of silence in English. How does one do that in German to an official of the secret police?

Then he said he understood I was in charge of the music. I answered that we did not have music. "No music in a church service? How can that be?" Obviously he thought I was lying or was just plain crazy. I tried to explain that, too, but not very convincingly.

Olga then cut through all this verbiage by saying, "We hold our services every Sunday at 11. Anyone is welcome. Perhaps you could come and see for yourself." In a simple way she had salvaged a difficult situation. How much I admired her for her astuteness. The officer seemed satisfied, and Olga and I left.

Another situation did not turn out so well. There were several young people in Germany who were close to Friends but not members. They were not encouraged at that time to join, as there was little to be gained and much to be lost by membership. So they remained friends of the Friends. Someone in Berlin developed a "concern" for those young people and a conference was arranged for them at Easter time.

66

The invitations were sent out by the secretary of the Berlin Young Friends group. She was Ruth Lilienthal and she signed her name in that way. A young man in Dresden received one of the invitations and asked permission to be away from his work. When asked why, he told his employer about the conference. The employer demanded proof and the young man showed his boss the invitation. Seeing the name on it, the employer suspected it was a Jewish name and took the invitation to the secret police, who got in touch with the Gestapo in Berlin.

Again I received a phone call and again I was in a quandary. But I decided to turn this matter over to the adviser of the Young Friends group as I had no responsibility for the upcoming conference. Eventually Ruth was summoned by the Gestapo and warned that another incident of this kind would bring dire consequences as she should have included the word "Sarah" in her signature, to indicate that she had some Jewish ancestry. Within a short time she went into hiding and stayed in hiding, like Anne Frank, for two years. At the close of the war she came to the United States, building a new life here as so many refugees have done.

Another curious contact with the government came at Christmas. Douglas Steere was in Germany, and he and I went to the tiny town of Stuben near the Swiss border. There we were joined by Greta Sumpf and we had a wonderfully refreshing time together. Then Greta returned to Vienna and Douglas crossed the border into Switzerland on his way back to the United States.

They both urged me to stay a few days for rest and recreation, and I accepted their suggestion gladly. Then came a phone call for Douglas from Berlin. I took it and discovered that the secret police wanted to know where Douglas Steere had been throughout the past week. When I retraced his travels, they seemed satisfied. Later I learned that there had been an attempt on Hitler's life and the police were checking Herr Steere's movement to determine whether he was involved in that plot. It was a fantastic idea, and Douglas and I have chuckled about it several times since. But at the time it was a very serious matter. Just why they had not implicated me, also, has always been a mystery.

SOME OF THE PEOPLE I KNEW IN GERMANY

The year 1940-1941 was a rugged time for a young man in his 20s to be in Nazi Germany. Some of the work was extremely demanding, and living there was not always easy, even for a foreigner. I was busy most of the time, but there were lonely evenings and weekends and times when I was homesick.

It was the friendships I formed there which sustained me most. Some of them were with Germans, such as the Hoffmans, Clara Schwanke, the Halles, and others. Among the younger Americans with whom I hobnobbed were Stewart Herman of the American Church and the U.S. Embassy, and Tracy Strong, a recent graduate of the Yale Divinity School who was working with the War Prisoners Committee of the International Y.M.C.A.

Much as the friendship of all those people meant to me, the close association with Howard Elkinton and Douglas Steere meant even more. Both of them were rare individuals and their extended visits meant much to me as well as to many other people.

Howard was an astute observer of the political scene and managed to persuade the American Friends Service Committee in Philadelphia to turn over the Berlin and Vienna Centers to German Friends because of the likelihood that the United States would eventually enter the war. I enjoyed his wry sense of humor, his interest in Quaker education and all facets of the Society of Friends, his growing interest in writing, and his knowledge of Germany, past and present.

Douglas' talents and interests were different. In a way they complemented each other. Douglas was intensely interested in the new movements within the churches of Germany and he sought out their leaders. He was also keenly interested in the small groups of Quakers in Scandinavia and was able to visit some of them while stationed in Berlin. His philosophical background, his speaking ability, and his knack of selecting a few key persons in German groups and working closely with them, intrigued and helped me. He, too, was a wonderful companion and an inspiration.

Alice Shaffer had left many friends in Germany and several of them took me in quickly because she was a friend of mine.

On my trips to various parts of Germany, I met many wonderful people. One was Wilhelm Mensching, whom I visited in a rural community where he was a Lutheran pastor. He was also head of the Fellowship of Reconciliation in Germany and had managed to keep it alive even during the Nazi regime. One of the many ways in which he worked was to produce a series of leaflets on outstanding thinkers and religious leaders, known as the Erbgut Heftchen or Heritage Leaflets. It was from that series that I got the idea for the Speaks Series of Biographical Booklets which I developed later in the United States.

On one of my trips I spoke on "Sources of Strength for Times Like These." In the course of that talk I mentioned two hymns — Luther's "A Mighty Fortress Is Our God" and Whittier's "Dear Lord and Father of Mankind." As I quoted some of the verses of the Whittier hymn, the face of one of the listeners lit up and her eyes gleamed. In her home that evening I told her that I had noticed the expression on her face and wondered if she would be willing to share with me the significance that that hymn had for her. "Yes," she said, "those words do have much meaning for me. I learned them in Woodbrooke years ago and during the months I was in concentration camp I used them every day as a morning prayer." After a pause she added, "Yes, those words have MUCH meaning for me."

Imagine sitting in a concentration camp, not knowing whether you would ever leave that spot alive, and you can understand a little better the meaning of the verses:

> Dear Lord and Father of Mankind,
> Forgive our feverish ways.
> Reclothe us in our rightful minds,

In purer lives Thy service find,
In deeper reverence, praise.

Drop Thy still dews of quietness,
Till all our strivings cease;
Take from our souls the strain and stress,
And let our ordered lives confess
The beauty of Thy peace.

Two other Quakers, Carl and Eva Hermann, lived in Mannheim but attended the Frankfurt Meeting when they could. He was a famous crystalographer. Both of them were active in work with Jewish people, including the sending of packages to those who had been deported to France. Eventually both of them were sent to jail, but both survived.

After that experience Eva wrote a brief but moving account of her months in prison called "In Prison, Yet Free." In it she wrote, "It may seem paradoxical for me to say that I would not have missed the experience of those two years of my life in a Nazi prison. But it is so." In a moving account she then told of her discovery of the power of prayer and other aspects of the spiritual life which brought her a deep inner joy.

One of the most wonderful women I have ever known was Margarethe Lachmund. She was on the International Center Committee and made frequent trips to Berlin from her home in Greifswald in northern Germany. She and her husband invited me to their home for a weekend before Christmas and there I learned that they had made plans to leave Nazi Germany but when the townspeople pleaded with them to stay, they had done so. Late in the spring of 1941 the Executive Committee of the German Yearly Meeting met and made detailed plans for the Quaker group to go underground in case that was necessary. It was an extraordinary document and I later learned that it was Margarethe who had devised it.

When I recall such people, I often think of Paul's letter to the Philippians in which he wrote, "I never think of you without thanking my God." Or I think of George Fox's statement that "The lives and conversations of Friends did preach."

MY RETURN TO THE UNITED STATES

In June of 1941 my year in Germany came to an end and Howard Elkinton and I returned together to New York City. When we arrived, Mother and Dad were at the wharf to meet me, unexpected on my part. With them were Barclay and Esther Jones of Friends Central School.

I was back home, but it was a different "I" from the person who had left the U.S.A. a year ago. My life had been profoundly altered.

National Legislation). When the Friends Meeting there had difficulty in paying Dad's meager salary, it was arranged for him to work part-time with Fred Libby. Libby was a former Congregational minister turned Quaker, an indomitable lobbyist and a forceful speaker. He was popular in the high schools in the District of Columbia but eventually was barred from speaking in them because of his pacifism. That experience made an indelible impression on me as Fred Libby was one of my boyhood heroes.

While I was in Earlham College, Margaret Dorland Webb applied for U.S. citizenship. She was the wife of the minister of the South Eighth Street Friends Meeting in Richmond, a member of a prominent English Quaker family, and a highly intelligent and educated woman. When her case came up in court, Dad and I were there. On one side of the courtroom were several immigrants and many representatives of the local American Legion and D.A.R. On the other side were several local Quakers, a few Friends from the national offices of the Five Years Meeting, and Mrs. Webb and members of her family.

With much help from the judge, all the immigrants passed their oral test in U.S. history and civics and were admitted as citizens. But Mrs. Webb, also an immigrant, was denied citizenship because she refused to promise to bear arms in time of war. To me there was something wrong with a system which would accept those almost illiterate immigrants and reject a highly intelligent woman like Margaret Webb.

Such were some of the factors in my becoming a pacifist.

THE C.P.S. CAMPS AT PATAPSCO AND POWELLSVILLE

In the fall of 1942 I entered my first Civilian Public Service camp. It was called Patapsco and was located in a state park near Baltimore. I did not enter it with glee, especially since my fiancee, Carol Richie, and I had just agreed to break our engagement. Since the camp was to be closed soon, there were few men there at the time, and a motley collection of campers it was.

Educationally they ranged from an illiterate Pennsylvania farmer to a well-known engineer with his doctoral degree. Most of the men were college graduates or had been studying in college before they were drafted. The average I.Q. was apparently very high.

Vocationally the most numerous were teachers. But in my barracks there were an aeronautical engineer, a salesman, an office worker, a roundhouse employee, a student of linguistics, an anthropologist, and two artists as well as others.

Religiously there were representatives of 25 Christian denominations, two Jews, and a few agnostics or atheists. The Quakers were the most numerous, but there were Baptists, Christadelphians, Jehovah's Witnesses, Methodists, and many other brands of Christians.

In their attitudes toward pacifism, a few were resisters on economic grounds. Most were objectors for religious reasons. A few weren't sure why they were in C.P.S. A couple of them eventually transferred to noncombatant service and others went the opposite direction, ending up in prison for conscience's sake.

The work was certainly not of national significance and no one found the camp life to his liking. By their stand on the war some had been alienated by their families and a few had lost their girl friends. All the Reubens in camp learned what a sad world this really is without any Rachels around. All the men had been torn from their jobs or their studies and wondered what would happen to them after the war. A large majority were accustomed to working with pens, typewriters or adding machines; working with picks, shovels and axes was therefore utterly alien to them.

In such situations someone always coins words to describe people or philosophical positions. There were the "lifers" or "Christers" who were supposed to enjoy C.P.S. and want to stay there forever. There were the "gropers," whose attitudes changed from day to day and even hour to hour. Finally there were the "gripers." They didn't like the camp. They didn't like many of their fellow campers. And psychologists would add that many of them didn't like themselves.

Originally the campers had tried to conduct the camp's business on the basis of a Quaker Meeting for Business. But most of the men had no idea of what that meant and had no practice in that form of business meeting. For a while they tried to combine "the sense of the Meeting" with parliamentary procedure but that was like mixing oil and water. Finally they resorted to parliamentary procedure, with the result that the camp split into factions, each trying to gather votes and garner power.

Many of the men were young and were wrestling with personal problems. Therefore they had little strength to concentrate on developing a sense of community. Especially among the older men there were a few who were more secure. If something was to be salvaged in that bleak situation, I felt that a tiny cell would have to be formed by those who were concerned about the religious basis of camp life.

Fortunately there were others who shared this concern. Gradually we developed a strong and closely-knit group of men who worshipped together almost every morning, came together from time to time to read and discuss devotional literature, and worshipped together on Sundays.

Our morning meditation group at Patapsco and later at Powellsville grew from three or four to 14 or 15, and our Sunday Meeting from 10 or 12 to 50, 60 or 70. Among the group were such fellows as Russ Freeman, Jack Hollister, Abe Kaminsky, Bob Leach, Howard Lutz, Don Mossholder, Ed Ramberg, John Musgrave, Bob Reitinger, Jim Seegers, Reed Smith, Ed Thatcher, and Paul Wilhelm.

When we moved that fall to an abandoned Civilian Conservation Corps camp at Powellsville, on the eastern shore of Maryland, our work was of greater significance. We were helping to clear a large area of trees and to construct a 14-mile canal to drain the land so that food could be grown on it. Years before, the C.C.C. campers had completed four miles of the canal and we were trying to complete it. Much of the land was swampy and we wore hip boots as we cut the small trees with axes and felled the large ones with two-man saws.

With our cell underway, my concern broadened to include concern for men of other religious persuasions. The Christadelphians and the Jehovah's Witnesses had their own groups, but the bulk of the Protestants had no service with which they were familiar. So we developed a Sunday evening service which featured hymn singing and short talks by the campers or visitors, and we even had an occasional liturgical service, conducted by the minister of the Episcopal church in nearby Salisbury.

My chief interest, however, was in a seminar in international relations. We met weekly for nearly a year, taking turns presenting papers. Occasionally we had visitors from outside the camp, but it was a remarkable group of men and we drew largely upon their talents. In it were Bill Vickrey, who had been in the State Department in Washington; Art Wiser, who had lived much of his life in India; Bob Levin, who had recently been the "city manager" of Antioch College; Jack Hollister, a teacher from George School; Bob Leach, who has spent most of his life at the International School in Geneva; Fran Marburg, who had been educated in Germany and at New College; and others.

After our year together we developed a 22-page guide to "Post-War Problems: A Study Outline for Individuals and Groups," which I edited as chairman of the seminar. That publication was used widely in C.P.S. camps and elsewhere.

Meanwhile many campers were leaving for special projects, such as work in mental hospitals, a smoke-jumpers unit, and work with the Coast and Geodetic Survey. The fellows in our seminar agreed to stay together for a year.

At the end of the year, I left Patapsco, pleased that the work I had done would be carried on by Grover Hartman, a fellow Hoosier who eventually became executive secretary of the Indianapolis Council of Churches.

The Overseas Training Unit at Earlham College
and Brief Sojourns in Other Camps

Officials in the American Friends Service Committee had been trying for a long time to get men released from the Quaker camps to prepare for relief work overseas. In the spring of 1943, A.F.S.C. officials persuaded Selective Service to release some men from the camps to study on four college campuses. One unit was to be located at Earlham College.

Eighteen men were selected for that unit and we arrived at Earlham in the summer of 1943, convinced that at last we were going to be doing work of national or even international significance.

But several Congressmen had a different slant on such work. The Senate approved the use of C.O.'s abroad, but a rider on a military appropriation bill in the House forbade C.O.'s to go abroad or to prepare themselves in the United States for such work.

News of that "rider" arrived at Earlham about the same time that we did. That was a bitter disappointment. There was one compensating factor; General Hershey ruled that we should continue our work for a "reasonable time," which turned out to be two months. That is the only time in our C.P.S. experience that we were grateful to the general.

At Earlham I had two unique experiences. One was taking French under the tutelage of my former Earlham classmate, Francis Hole. The other was teaching a course in Quakerism to the members of the C.P.S. unit and to most of the summer school students.

Our unit there consisted of the following men: Elton Atwater, Kermit Bonner, Edwin Bronner, George Cates, George Haight, Timothy Haworth, myself, Roy Kepler, John McAllister, William McLaughlin, John Olson, Charles Piersol, Kenneth Roberts, Ross Sanderson, Samuel Snipes, Marshall Sutton, Robert Turner and Darrell Randall.

Several of those men decided to stay together after the Earlham interlude and that fall we went to West

Campton, New Hampshire. I was in a sidecamp most of the time, painting the buildings of the National Park Service. On the long trips back to the main camp over the weekends, I enjoyed the flaming foliage of a New England autumn and some magnificent views of The Old Man of the Mountain.

Late that fall we transferred for a few weeks to a Mennonite camp at Luray, Virginia. In some ways that was like going to a foreign country for nearly all the campers were Mennonites from Lancaster County, Pennsylvania, and the camp was like a "colony" of that part of the U.S.A.

When our unit arrived there, we decided to keep relatively quiet as we were, in a sense, guests of theirs for a short time only. But we discovered that it was difficult and then impossible, for our sense of justice was soon offended. We learned, for example, that one camper with a car, who had been given the concession to drive campers to and from the railroad station, was piling eight and ten men in his car and charging them $2 each for a short ride. We noted, too, that some beautiful lumber given to the camp for the use of all the men was being sold rather than given away. And the night watchman had worked for months without a night off and nobody had protested that injustice. So we spoke out and some changes were made, although not all we suggested.

As Christmas approached, the men in our unit decided to sponsor a simple Christmas party with an exchange of inexpensive gifts. Some of the Mennonite campers objected to any celebration of Christmas as a heathen practice. Therefore a few of them were elated on Christmas day when we were called out to fight a forest fire, the first in that region in months. That was God's retribution, some of them said. But that night we had our big Christmas dinner — and our gift exchange.

THE DISTRICT TRAINING SCHOOL

In peace time it is difficult to find qualified persons to work in institutions for the mentally handicapped; in wartime it is doubly difficult. During World War II some of those institutions appealed to Selective Service for the help of men from the C.P.S. camps. Consequently our unit moved early in 1944 to the District Training School, an institution for mentally retarded boys and girls from the District of Columbia. At the time we were there, it housed 650 such persons.

My job was with the younger and the more intelligent boys. A half dozen of them attended a school on the grounds which went through the third grade, which was as far as anyone in that institution could go scholastically. My charges ranged in I.Q., on individually administered tests, from 17 to 48 (90 to 110 is the average for most persons). I was an assistant to Mrs. Musgrove, the "house mother," who was really interested in the boys.

Most of the time I worked with the youngest ones. The "house father" was limited in ability and kept order by having the little fellows sit in adult chairs all day with their feet dangling. In front of them he placed an older boy, equipped with a rubber hose to use if anyone tried to escape.

It was not a promising situation, but I was determined to make the most of it. Since there were no toys or play equipment, I prevailed upon my friends to send paper, stuffed animals, wooden beads or anything they could collect. The house father was vehemently opposed at first to letting them get out of their chairs, so I gave them stuffed animals to play with, developed hand games, and played victrola records when he was not around. Gradually I won permission to take them on walks or to let them play on the floor for short intervals.

Soon I learned some of the limitations of the mentally retarded. But I also learned some things they could do. One of my most thrilling experiences was to hear the solos and chorus work of the "inmates" who had been trained by Bill Reese, one of the members of our unit who would later become chairman of the music department at Haverford College.

In our spare time several of us continued our

preparation for work overseas, aided by our able director, Jack Petherbridge, and our industrious and imaginative educational director, Elton Atwater. I decided, however, that we were not likely to be used abroad, so I began a reading program on my own, focusing on international education.

THE HUMAN GUINEA PIG EXPERIMENT AT YALE UNIVERSITY

After approximately a year in the District Training School, I was ready to move. I had learned a lot but was restless and eager for something different.

By that time Selective Service was beginning to use men from the C.P.S. camps and units in human guinea pig experiments, and a new one was planned at Yale University in which infectious hepatitis would be studied under the auspices of the Epidemiological Board of the U.S. Army.

The American Friends Service Committee was finally developing the idea of special camps or units in which men of similar interests would study together in their spare time. So these two approaches were combined and preference was given in the Yale unit to men who thought they wanted to teach. I was asked to head that part of the Yale project.

In the first experiment, I was one of the "controls," and as my special work project, I assisted Dr. Catherine Miles in some of her research. She was already famous as one of the co-directors of the Terman-Miles Study of Gifted Children conducted in California. So I had an opportunity to work with children on the other end of the scale from those in the District Training School.

On some evenings and over the weekends a small group of us explored teaching as a profession. Often we were helped by well-known educators who came for short periods to work with us.

In the second experiment I contracted hepatitis and was a mighty sick patient. One night I was so tired of the shots in my arm and the feeding through a rubber tube that I refused to swallow the tube. The young doctor connected with the experiment pled with me, threatened me and tried to bribe me, but I still refused. Finally he decided to leave me alone for a few minutes and by the time he had returned I was willing to swallow that long, slippery piece of rubber once more and be fed.

I was flat on my back for weeks and when I was allowed to leave the bed, I looked like a barrel because they had fed us on a high protein diet to see if that would help in our recovery.

The experiment was far from pleasant, but it was important. We had helped the doctors and the medical profession in general, and we had helped to save lives rather than to destroy them. At last we had been given significant work.

Coshocton, Big Flats, and My Discharge from C.P.S.

After the guinea pig experiment, I was sent to Coshocton, Ohio, where the campers were working with Soil Conservation specialists on an erosion project. But my time there was short. On March 1, 1946, Steve Carey and I closed the last door in a little ceremony which terminated Coshocton as a C.P.S. camp.

From there I was sent across the eastern half of the United States to a similar camp in Big Flats, New York. From there I was discharged one day after my arrival. What a use of taxpayers' money!

The experience in C.P.S. had been traumatic for some men. A few were destroyed by it and some were hurt by it, at least temporarily. Eventually many of the "gripers" and some of the "gropers" transferred to camps financed by the government. Those men had not been happy in camps run by religious groups and they felt that the government had a responsibility to support and run the C.O. camps. They had a point, although the government had not been willing to do that when the C.P.S. camps were organized.

Early in the days of C.P.S. I had pled with Paul Furnas, Paul French, and other top officials whom I knew, to develop different kinds of camps. Some would have been primarily for those whose pacifism was religiously-based. Others would have been for those who were war resisters on economic or philosophical grounds. I also urged those men to develop camps with special interests, such as our international relations group at Powellsville. It was my contention that the early Quakers in Pennsylvania had killed The Holy Experiment by undue generosity to persons who did not believe in what Penn and his friends were trying to do. Those early Quakers were too few in number, too weak in their faith, and too poor as administrators to make a success of that Experiment, especially when they were overwhelmed by persons who were not in accord with it. In the end the Quakers were outvoted in the legislature and withdrew when the lawmakers appropriated funds for the French and Indian War. I felt that history was being repeated in the C.P.S. experiment. It is one thing to be generous; it is another thing to be generous to the point that you destroy what you have worked long and hard to create.

In the latter months of C.P.S., an induction camp was established, several specialized camps and units created, and government camps organized. Other improvements were made, but they were made too late in many instances.

Nevertheless those years were fruitful for many of us. In an article in *The American Friend* in 1946, I wrote about some of the benefits I thought I had derived from my years in camps and units. The article was entitled "As C.P.S. Ends."

Thrust into a new situation with a wide variety of human beings, I thought I had learned much about myself, my strengths and my weaknesses. I had certainly made many new friends and I had gained respect for people with different views from mine. In addition, I had gained a sense of vocational direction. I felt, too, that I had become more socially conscious and that my faith had been tested and deepened. In addition, I had met and learned from many outstanding persons — people like Roland Bainton, E. Stanley Jones, Haradas Mazundar, Arthur Morgan, A.J. Muste, Frank Olmstead, Irene Pickard, Bayard Rustin, Ruth Seabury and Katherine Whiteside Taylor, all of whom had come to some camp or unit as resource persons.

In retrospect those were not wasted years. Despite all the difficulties and disillusion, they were profitable years for me as well as for many others.

CHAPTER 7

The Religious Society of Friends and My Part in the Quaker Adventure

What pictures flash onto the screen in your mind when the word "Quaker" is mentioned? A heavy-set man with a broadbrimmed hat and a plain coat? A woman with a Quaker bonnet and a shawl? Some names like William Penn, John Woolman or Lucretia Mott — or Rufus Jones, Clarence Pickett or Howard and Anna Cox Brinton? The American Friends Service Committee or the Friends Committee on National Legislation? Or some Quaker you know?

In my mind there are thousands of slides of Quakers, Quaker Meetings, Quaker schools and colleges, Quaker organizations and Quaker committees, because my identification with Friends has been lifelong and far-flung. I have been a member of six yearly meetings and a visitor in at least 12 others in the United States. I have lived within the limits of London Yearly Meeting and of the French Yearly Meeting and worked closely with German Friends. And I have visited Friends groups in other parts of Europe, the Middle East, Africa, Asia, Latin America and North America.

In addition I have attended a Quaker school and college, taught in two others, and served on the Boards of Trustees of three more. And I have spoken fairly widely to Friends groups and written extensively for and about Friends.

89

George Fox and the Early Quakers

The Religious Society of Friends is a tiny group, limited largely to the Anglo-Saxon world, with only 200,000 members, of whom approximately 120,000 live in the United States. Yet it has had an influence for 300 years far beyond that of any religious group which is similar in size.

In order to understand the Religious Society of Friends today and to suggest what it could be tomorrow, it is important to understand its past. Telescoped, the story goes something like this:

Seventeenth-century England was a time of religious turmoil and spiritual searching. Early in that century George Fox was born. As a young man the world seemed baffling to him and all his attempts to create order out of the chaos in his mind failed. Then something happened. He described that "something" in unforgettable language: "And when all my hopes in them (the preachers) and in all men were gone, . . .I heard a voice which said, 'There is one, even Christ Jesus, that can speak to thy condition,' and when I heard it, my heart did leap for joy."

That experience and others like it led to his spiritual and physical integration and drove him out to tell others that they, too, could know God "experimentally," for it was clear to him that "every man was enlightened by the Divine Light of Christ."

Clad in leather clothes, Fox set out on journeys that took him to many parts of England, to Germany and the Netherlands, to the Barbadoes, and to several of the American colonies. Everywhere he proclaimed his message of the transforming power of God. Religion to Fox was not a creed or an organization, but a life. In such a life people received their power directly from God, rather than through intermediaries. Then they turned that power into day-to-day Christian living. Religion was therefore a twofold relationship — a vertical relationship with God and a horizontal relationship with other people.

Fox referred to them as the inward and the outward states.

These ideas were not new. Fox was not a religious revolutionist. He was a religious revivalist struggling to bring back the power and authenticity of early Christianity.

But the church leaders of his day considered Fox a revolutionist. Where they proclaimed the doctrine of human depravity, he proclaimed the possibility of human perfection. Where they declared the doctrine of the elect, he declared that all men (and women) are elect. Where they believed that revelation had stopped hundreds of years ago, he believed that it was a contemporary fact and that everyone could have revelations from God. Where they believed in the supremacy of the Bible, he believed in the supremacy of the Inner Light of Christ. Where they were chiefly concerned with the future world, he was primarily interested in the here and now. Where they insisted upon belief in a formal creed, he held such a creed unnecessary. And whereas they upheld the sacraments as an essential part of Christianity, he considered them substitutes for the one and only sacrament, a Christian life.

Fox and the other early Friends believed that people could hear God best in silence. Sermons, music, a beautiful altar and stained glass windows were hindrances rather than helps to worship, distracting the worshipers so that they could not hear God.

Those early Friends believed in individual and family worship, but they felt that group worship was equally important and often created a heightened sense of the Divine Presence. From this came the Quaker idea of group worship — not of silent meetings but of meetings on the basis of silence, of openness, of searching, and of expectancy in Divine Guidance. That was a radical departure from the accepted forms of Christian worship in their day and even now.

Individuals in any religious movement can outrun the supposed leadings of the Spirit and in early Quakerism there were several such instances. Therefore the leadings of individuals needed to be tempered by the leadings of the group. Fox realized that anarchy would not enhance the Quaker movement, so, in another "leading" or a stroke of genius, he devised a special method of organizing early Friends.

If God led people in their religious experiences, He could also guide them in their temporal affairs. So Fox suggested that Friends in a community band themselves together in small fellowship groups or societies of friends. In those tiny "cells" they would carry on the business of the group. Such meetings would be conducted very much like a Meeting for Worship. In them women and children as well as men would participate. Decisions would be made by the entire group under the leadership of the Spirit. Therefore no votes would be taken, leaving disgruntled minorities. In recent years the word consensus has been used, but that is not what early Friends were trying to achieve. They were trying to come to right decisions through listening to God's will.

That is often a slow and painful process, but it is an incredibly successful way of doing business when the group really searches for the "sense of the Meeting" and an able clerk (or chairman) is sensitive in handling the business.

Most of the religious movements in 17th-century England collapsed. But the Quaker movement survived because it had an organizational structure as well as a spiritual message.

Its survival and growth was also due to an able group of ministers who traveled "under concern." Some Friends today do not like to think of them as evangelists, but they certainly were.

Early Quakers were deeply involved in their own spiritual movement, but they were also socially concerned. They worked valiantly for better conditions in prisons; for peace; and especially in the American colonies, for improved race relations, first with the Indians and later with Negroes. Thus early Quakers were social activists.

With the exception of Fox, all of those early leaders

were also highly educated. Several of them combined rational thought with religious experience in a remarkable way.

Those early Quaker leaders were also well acquainted with the Bible. It was a part of their rich background for the ministry. Important as it was, however, they subordinated the authority of the Bible to the authority of direct experience — The Inner Light of Christ, as they called it.

Friends also had testimonies on simple living and on equality. They accorded equal rights to women, something very radical in England then.

It seems to me that those early Friends combined in a remarkable way seven major testimonies, as depicted in this simple chart:

Ration-alism and Education	+Social Concern	+Simplicity	+The Historic Christ and The Inner Christ	+Equal-ity	+The Bible	+Evangel-ism and Missions

Friends for 300 Years

Better than any historian, Howard Brinton succeeded in simplifying Quaker history without distorting it. In his penetrating and perceptive volume on *Friends for 300 Years* he divided Quaker history into four periods:

1. The heroic or apostolic period. About 1650-1700.
2. The period of cultural creativeness. About 1650-1800.
3. The period of conflict and decline. About 1800-1900.
4. The period of modernism. From 1900 on.

Unfortunately few groups are self-renewing. They tend to stagnate. So it was with Friends. Gradually the delicate balance between individuality and community was upset. So was the balance between tradition and innovation. Pressures for conformity to sterile standards prevailed and people who diverged even slightly from those established norms were "disowned," which is a pleasant way of saying they were thrown out of the Society.

Then came the divisions within the Society of Friends in the United States.

The first was the Hicksite-Orthodox schism in the 1820 s. There have been several interpretations of that division, but most writers now agree that it started as a revolt of the rank and file against the elders and of rural Friends against city Friends (who tended to be wealthier and more conservative). In the beginning both retained the original type of Quaker worship and both emphasized simplicity and equality. When that split occurred, the largest groups in the Philadelphia, Baltimore and New York areas were Hicksites.

Then came a second split which started in New England in 1846 and spread to other areas, but only among the Orthodox. That schism was precipitated by the visit of Joseph John Gurney, a prominent English Quaker and a brother of the famous prison reformer, Elizabeth Fry. Gurney was a scholar, an ardent student of the Bible, an advocate of higher education, and an evangelical. Opposing him was a New England Quaker named John Wilbur, who championed the doctrine of the Inner Light and opposed the changes and innovations of Gurney, asserting that Bible schools and lectures were too premeditated and smacked of worldly preparation for Meetings for Worship. Thus the controversy became known as the Wilburite-Gurneyite division. Small groups of Quakers in Rhode Island, North Carolina, Indiana, Ohio, North Carolina and Iowa, plus a larger group in Philadelphia, became Wilburites. The larger group of Orthodox Friends, primarily in the midwest, became Gurneyites.

For a long time Philadelphia had been the hub of American Quakerism. As Friends moved farther west, however, they became more and more removed from the hub. Many of their Meetings lacked a prophetic ministry and began to decline. In an effort to bolster their dwindling congregations, Quakers began to ape the Methodists and other Protestant groups, introducing music, organizing young people's groups, and hiring ministers. Eventually most Quaker groups in the middle west and west became pastoral meetings. Many of them were the only places of worship in an area and therefore served as community churches.

In 1902 most of the Gurneyite Quakers banded together to form the Five Years Meeting of Friends (called now the Friends United Meeting), with its headquarters in Richmond, Indiana. This is the largest group in the United States and includes groups in Cuba, Jamaica, Mexico, and East Africa which were formed as a result of Quaker missionaries.

Several thousand Quakers, however, did not feel that the Five Years Meeting was "sound" theologically or evangelical enough and either did not join it or eventually withdrew from it. Recently they have organized what is called the Evangelical Friends Church. Its chief strength is in Ohio, Kansas and Oregon.

The third group of Friends today is the Friends General Conference with headquarters in Philadelphia. It comprises the bulk of Friends who maintain the original mode of worship on the basis of silent expectation. That group also stresses, even more than the others, social action.

The small group of Wilburites maintain some contact with each other but have no national organization.

In the last few years several Quaker groups have joined both the Friends United Meeting and the Friends General Conference.

The story of these various schisms is a tragic one. Fortunately, however, there has been a movement toward cooperation among the various groups in recent years. Today most American Quakers are working together in the American Friends Service Committee, in the Friends World Committee, and in the Friends Committee on National Legislation.

At the risk of oversimplification, here is a chart showing the various branches of American Quakerism and the parts of the total testimony which they have stressed. Readers should note that the unified testimony on Christ is divided in this chart into two testimonies.

WORLDVIEW

Ration- alism and Education	+Social Concern	+Sim- plicity	+The Inward Christ	+The Historic Christ	+Equal- ity	+The Bible	+Evangel- ism and Missions
			Wilburites		Gurneyites		Evangelicals

HICKSITES   ORTHODOX

My Experience with Different Kinds of Quakers

Fortunately I have had experiences in the United States with almost all kinds of Quakers. I say "fortunately" because I think my life has been enriched by contact with each group.

My earliest years were spent almost exclusively with Orthodox Friends of the Gurneyite group. When I went to Westtown at the age of 10, I had never attended a Friends Meeting on the basis of expectant silence. I fully expected a piano or an organ to be pulled out of the wall and tried to figure out where it was hidden. Westtown was run by the Wilburite-Orthodox group and so I had several years of contacts with that branch. That contact continued when I taught at Friends Select School.

Friends Central was run by Hicksite Friends so my Quaker circle was enlarged when I taught there. And by choice I joined a United Meeting, the Providence Road Meeting, near Media.

During the period of my life in Philadelphia I began to realize that there were still a few differences between the two Philadelphia Quaker groups, but not many. In the early 1940s they were gradually coming together and a committee was formed to consider organic union. I was fortunate in being asked to serve on that committee, although my departure for a C.P.S. camp meant that I attended only a few of their meetings. But that union was eventually accomplished.

And when I moved to New York City, a similar movement was underway, eventually bringing about the union of the Orthodox and Hicksite groups in that region.

For many years I have tried to build bridges between different kinds of Quakers. In my booklet on *Meditations*

96

Around the World, printed in 1958, I wrote briefly on "Learning from All Kinds of Quakers," as follows:

Gurneyites, Hicksites, and Wilburites. Five Years Meeting Friends, General Conference Friends, Evangelical Friends, and Independents. Birthright Friends, Convinced Friends, and Overconvinced Friends. It makes one's head ache to try to understand the many Quaker groups, and one's heart bleed to realize that such divisions exist.

Quakerism today is like a good-sized plot of ground which has been divided among several sons and daughters, each inheriting a small section of the original plot. These strips are too small to cultivate properly alone, and yet people do not seem to be able to farm them cooperatively.

What a Society we would have if we could work together, learning from each other and using the talents of each group. In such a Society we would utilize the zeal, sacrificial giving, and concern for the spreading of the gospel, of Evangelical Friends. We would profit from the mission work, the concern for children and young people, the talents of many pastors, the network of colleges, and the broad base of membership of Five Years Meeting Friends. And we would all gain from the highly educated, upper middle-class membership of the Friends General Conference and of Independent Friends, with their emphasis upon worship on the basis of silence and their interest in social service.

What a Society of Friends that combination would make!

A VISIT WITH RUFUS JONES

In what was probably the most powerful message of his long and useful life, Rufus Jones addressed all Friends in the United States in the early 1940s with the question, "Are We Ready?" He had a vision of a great people to be gathered and wondered if Friends were prepared to speak to their condition.

That message moved me deeply and I had such a strong desire to talk with him that I wrote and asked if I might come for a brief visit. He replied, "Do come. You are most welcome." So I journeyed to Haverford College from my C.P.S. camp and met him in his home for a couple of hours.

We talked first about the idea of small groups of Friends visiting the men in the C.P.S. camps and about encouraging communication among different groups of Friends, especially in Ohio. I had recently taken my furlough from camp to visit with different groups in that state to promote dialogue among them. He spoke frankly about the strengths and weaknesses of several prominent Friends to undertake such a mission.

Later he expressed disappointment about the response of many older Friends to his call for renewal. But he was encouraged by the cooperation between Wilburite and Five Years Meeting Friends in Iowa in the revival of the Scattergood School. In that connection he referred to the little group of Wilburite Friends in Iowa as "about the best on our planet."

I asked him about the decision in some groups of Friends not to "record" ministers and he replied that he thought that was a mistake. In his own case, he pointed out, he had not expected to be recorded, but that expression of confidence in his gifts had meant a great deal to him. In general, he said, the recording of ministers was beneficial.

He also commented that he hoped some Friends college would establish a training school for ministers. Actually such a plan was developed years later with the establishment at Earlham College of the Earlham School of Religion.

In discussing promising areas in the U.S.A. for Friends, he cautioned against concentrating on any one region or group of people, such as university groups, saying that it was important to bear witness in many divergent groups as one never knew where revitalization might take place.

When I asked about the need for a rebirth of a prophetic ministry, he answered that that was "the greatest need of the Society of Friends in our day."

At the end of our conversation we had a brief period of silent worship and a prayer. For me this was a memorable visit with one of the great leaders in Quaker history.

THE FAMILY OF FRIENDS AROUND THE WORLD

Because of my interest in international affairs, it was natural that I developed a particular concern for the world-wide Society of Friends.

This probably began with my appointment as a delegate from Indiana Yearly Meeting to the Friends World Conference, held in 1937 at Swarthmore College. Dad was also a delegate and Grandpa Kenworthy attended some of the meetings, so that event involved three generations of our family. In addition, I served as a special correspondent for the *Philadelphia Record.*

My years in England, France and Germany also brought me in contact with Friends in other countries, as well as my visits in many parts of the world.

For several years I served on the Friends World Committee for Consultation and took part in many of its meetings, including conferences in The Netherlands and in Kenya, and attendance at the World Conference in Oxford, England, in 1952.

In addition, I served for several years on the committee which consulted with the personnel of the Quaker Program at the U.N. in New York City.

SOME SUBSEQUENT WRITINGS ON QUAKERISM

As I visited various types of Quakers I was struck by the puerility of many messages in silent Meetings and of many sermons in Friends churches. Perhaps the strongest religious statement I ever wrote was sketched on scraps of paper on a train between Philadelphia and New York in 1945. The article which emerged was called "Message-Bearers Needed" and was printed in several Quaker publications. Two paragraphs from that article indicate its major emphasis, as follows:

> The Society of Friends stands now on the threshold of a revitalization as an instrument of God. Its rebirth must come through scores of reborn men and women. And its rebirth will come only when a vital, living ministry arises among us. . . .
>
> Too long we have dared God to make ministers of us, until our resistance was so great that God could not make use of us as His fellow workers. Instead we must strive for that spirit out of which a living ministry will arise spontaneously. We must be open and sensitive, even desirous of the gift in the ministry, and dedicated enough to prepare ourselves for such work.

99

Throughout my life that theme of the centrality of the ministry has been a continuing concern.

As a teacher in two Quaker schools and as a member of a C.P.S. camp, I had been appalled by the lack of explanations of our method of worship and of personalized accounts of what individuals do in a Meeting for Worship. Douglas Steere and Tom Kelly had written such accounts, but no one had written especially for young people.

As I worked in the swamps of eastern Maryland, bits and pieces of such an account came to me and I jotted them down in a little notebook I carried in my hip pocket. I had recently been rescued from drowning by my good friend, Peg Wagner, so that experience was still with me as I wrote. The article was called "Going to Meeting" and was published in *The Friend* and later as a Pennsbury leaflet. The opening paragraphs read as follows:

> Learning to worship in silence is very much like learning to swim. Some people need no instruction. They grasp intuitively the art of silent worship. As soon as they enter the silence, they sense what to do. They relax physically, stretch themselves out spiritually, and feel the power in and around them. They revel in their experience of group meditation and come out of the Meeting for Worship spiritually refreshed, better able to live truly Christian lives.
>
> Others have more difficulty in learning to worship in this way. They seem to fight the silence as an inexperienced swimmer fights the sea. They feel as if they had been carried out to where the water is deepest and then thrown overboard, without any idea of what to do. Only the handshake at the end of Meeting saves them from "drowning" in the silence.

Then I suggested some of the ways in which people prepare for Meeting, comparing that to the approach to a diving board. Several paragraphs were then devoted to the "different strokes" people use in silence, from an opening prayer to reviewing the past week's activities. I reminded readers, however, that as one meditates and prays, one should remember that worship is a conversation rather than a monologue and that worshipers should be quiet and listen, just as the expert swimmer often floats in the water.

Here is the closing paragraph of that article:

Throughout any period of worship it is well to bear in mind the thought expressed so beautifully by the English painter, J. Doyle Penrose, in the painting known as "The Presence in the Midst." In it he portrays a Quaker Meeting House in the early days of Quakerism, with the men in their broad-brimmed hats on one side of the room. . .and the women in their plain bonnets on the other. Through the lattice windows between the facing benches streams the sunlight. And in the sunlight the artist has shown a figure in dim outline, symbolizing the Spirit of Christ in their midst. In every Meeting for Worship that Spirit is there for those who would have communion with Him.

In 1943 I had written an article for *The Friend* on "The Society of Friends in 1968," a projection of what I hoped we would be able to accomplish by then. Later that article was rewritten and appeared as a Pennsbury leaflet with the title "The Society of Friends in 1970." My hope was that by then we would be a deeply religious society, an articulate society, a united society, a world society, an inclusive society, and an adventurous society.

Perhaps my expectations were too great. As a young man I probably did not realize how slowly changes come or how much resistance there often is to change. But, perhaps, as Elton Trueblood suggested at the World Conference of Friends in Oxford, England, in 1952, "We are guilty of treason to a great trust."

In 1970 I was not ready to make an inventory of the gains and losses in the quarter century since I had written that article. But in 1974 I did write an account of "The State of the Religious Society of Friends in the U.S.A. in 1974," which was published in *Quaker Life*.

In that article I pointed out some of the gains in the last quarter-century and more. Among them I mentioned the fact that all kinds of Friends had wrestled with the question of a dynamic, relevant Christian-Quaker message for our time and that retreat centers like Powell House in New York and Ben Lomond in California had been established. I pointed out that Pendle Hill had grown in influence and that the Earlham School of Religion had been founded. Different types of Quakers had finally begun a dialogue, starting with the historic conference in St. Louis in 1970, and Friends in New England, New York, Baltimore and Philadelphia had become united after a long interval. In addition, many new Meetings had been started and several new yearly meetings formed, extending Quakerism in the U.S.A.

Furthermore several new Friends schools and two colleges had been started and several older institutions had rediscovered their unique Quaker role. A few "intentional communities" had been formed and several camps, especially for young people, started. Many Friends, I wrote, had taken part in the civil rights movement and in antiwar demonstrations, reexamining their views on various forms of protest.

In addition, I mentioned that more and more Quakers had become involved in the work of the American Friends Service Committee and the Friends Committee on National Legislation. Some Friends had rediscovered the ancient Quaker testimony about prisons and many had become involved in work with the United Nations.

To me all these trends indicated that there was tremendous vitality in the Society of Friends in 1974.

But I also pointed out some of the losses, some areas of stagnation, and some of the unfulfilled promises. I stated that we were still a small, splintered society, faced with an identity crisis, with too few Friends involved in a search for a message for today and tomorrow, based on some areas of common agreement. And I stated that because much of our worship was perfunctory and peripheral, much of our social action was "creaturely activity" rather than religiously-motivated concern. I maintained, also, that we were better at applying band-aids to a sick society than at diagnosing its ills and prescribing preventive medicine.

I stated my contention that we needed to become evangelical without becoming evangelistic, proclaiming the Good Tidings that Christ lived and lives in everyone, everywhere, and that he is able to help transform individuals and groups. I also maintained that we were still predominantly an Anglo-Saxon, white, conservative, exclusive society.

At the request of the Friends United Meeting in 1975, I wrote a pamphlet on the "Friends Peace Testimony," and added four more leaflets in the Speaks Series, which included Kenneth Boulding, Howard Brinton, Douglas Steere, and Elton Trueblood, bringing to 16 the Quaker titles in that series.

Perhaps it is appropriate to conclude this chapter with a section from a talk I gave at the 100th anniversary of the 15th Street Meeting House in New York City, in 1961, which I think still applies to Quakers at their best. Since many non-Friends were in attendance for that celebration, I included a section on "A Message to Spiritual Seekers" in my remarks. It reads as follows:

If you consider creeds archaic and even intellectually dishonest, Friends offer you the creedless church, a spiritual fellowship of those who seek direct contact with God, with Jesus Christ as their Guide and Teacher.

If you reject materialism and secularism as the goals of life, Friends remind you of their basic belief that the purpose of life is primarily spiritual and that individual and group worship are central in lives worth living.

If you are caught in a web of anxieties and tensions, Friends welcome you to their quiet worship where they seek together the spiritual resources which enable people to live more calmly and more creatively in this confused and chaotic world.

If you are distressed by the impersonalism of our large metropolitan areas, Friends point out that their Meetings are intended as "homes away from home" and their groups small fellowships of seekers for the realities of life.

If you shudder at the might of the world, Friends urge you to join them in seeking ways to prevent conflicts and promote international understanding and cooperation.

If you lament the lack of pioneering enterprises and the retreat into political, economic, educational, and religious orthodoxies, Friends invite you to share with them in a variety of ways to relieve human suffering and confront the basic causes of maladjustments in individuals and in society.

You will not find that we have discovered a great many of the answers to the riddle of life, but we do believe you will learn that we have found some satisfying answers. We trust, too, that you will discover that we are seeking diligently and prayerfully for God's leadership in our lives.

Such are a few of my thoughts on the fragile but

remarkable Religious Society of Friends and some of my activities in it over a period of many years. In fact I have attempted to undergird all my activities with the central beliefs of Friends. In a sense I have had two vocations — teacher and Quaker.

CHAPTER 8

Helping To Create an International Educational Organization: The Formation of UNESCO

What would you do if you were asked to help form an international educational organization which was to be part of the United Nations? What purposes would you stress? What programs would you propose? What personnel would you want to recruit?

Such were some of the questions on my mind as I flew from New York City to London early in 1946 to become a member of the Secretariat of the Preparatory Commission of the United Nations Educational, Scientific, and Cultural Organization, known almost from the start as UNESCO.

In my hand I clutched a thin booklet which contained the Constitution of the organization, reading and re-reading it in order to gain a better understanding of what UNESCO was expected to do.

The Preamble was filled with as many "thats" as there are "begats" in the Old Testament. But there were some stirring statements which followed the "thats." Especially provocative was the opening phrase:

"that since wars begin in the minds of men, it is in the minds of men that the defences of peace must be constructed."

Over and over in the coming months I would hear that phrase repeated. But I would also hear it attacked as a

105

false explanation of the cause of war, inasmuch as some people contended that wars arise in the stomachs of men rather than in their minds.

Further on was the statement:

> "that ignorance of each other's ways and lives has been a common cause, throughout history, of that suspicion and mistrust between the peoples of the world through which their differences have all too often broken into war. . . ."

I wondered about that, doubting that knowledge about people guaranteed understanding.

The Preamble was filled with high-sounding phrases. But could hardhitting programs be developed to give substance to those idealistic statements? I believed they could. I recalled Thoreau's remark that "If you have built castles in the air, your work need not be lost. That is where they should be. Now put the foundations under them." Our job in the Secretariat would be to make blueprints for such foundations, and later construct them.

In that document I also found a section on the purposes of UNESCO. It was a little more concrete. I re-read it and drew a simple chart like this:

The purpose of UNESCO is
to contribute to
PEACE and SECURITY
through
Education, Science, and Culture
by

1) advancing the mutual knowledge and understanding of peoples.
2) giving fresh impulse to popular education and the spread of culture.
3) maintaining, increasing, and diffusing knowledge.

The Road to UNESCO

With me I also took an abbreviated history of international education which I had drafted some months before my trip. I knew that UNESCO was something new but that the ideas behind its formation were old. The road to UNESCO was a long, long trail winding over the centuries. On it many people had trod. Some of them were the great religious and philosophical leaders. Others were the professors in the ancient universities of Asia, Africa and the Middle East, whose knowledge belonged to people everywhere.

Then there had been men and women who had dreamed of some kind of international bureau of education — people like John Amos Comenius, Marc Antoine Jullien and Herman Molkenboer.

I knew, too, that when the League of Nations was established, Fannie Fern Andrews and others had lobbied for an International Office of Education. Their plan was never adopted, but an International Institute of Intellectual Cooperation had been established. However, its yearly budget was only $14,000 and its secretariat consisted of one person. Its intent was to deal with intellectual affairs at the very top rather than at the grass roots.

Then came the International Bureau of Education, established in Geneva in 1925 because of disappointment with the I.I.I.C. At first it was a bureau of interested individuals, but by 1929 it had become an intergovernmental organization with strong support from the Swiss government.

During World War II several of the governments-in-exile were located in London and their Ministers of Education worked together on common problems of reconstructing their school systems after the war. From those deliberations emerged the idea of a United Nations organization for educational and cultural reconstruction.

The hopes of those Ministers of Education and of many other individuals and groups moved farther toward reality when the United Nations Conference in San Francisco recommended in 1945 the formation of an international organization in education and culture.

Thus the trails of creative educational thinkers turned into a highway which led in 1946 to UNESCO House in Paris.

107

A Construction Worker on the UNESCO Highway

Some readers may wonder how any individual became associated with UNESCO in its early days. A brief account of my experience may serve as a partial answer to that question.

Shortly after my return to the United States from Germany in 1941, I reviewed Walter Kotschnig's *Slaves Need No Leaders*, an account of youth in Nazi Germany. Included in my review were references to recent events there and Dr. Kotschnig asked me about my sources. That led to an exchange of letters and a list of books he sent me on comparative education. That list became an individualized reading course for me.

In the coming months a movement was developing in the United States for the formation of an international office of education. Several groups supported that idea and eventually they came together in a Liaison Committee, headed by Dr. Grayson Kefauver, Dean of the School of Education at Stanford University. They held three conferences in the U.S.A., and I was able to attend the one at Hood College in Maryland in 1944.

When my years in the Civilian Public Service were about to end, I wrote Walter Kotschnig in London, asking about the possibility of work with the Preparatory Commission for UNESCO. He had left UNESCO by the time my letter arrived, but he was succeeded by Dr. Howard E. Wilson, under whom I had studied at Harvard. Howard cabled me, inviting me to come for a period of three months. Soon I was on my way to London for what turned out to be almost three strenuous but exciting years.

The Preparatory Commission of UNESCO

London in those days was cold and dreary. All around us was the evidence of the devastation wrought by the bombs of the luftwaffe. Places to live and places to work were extremely difficult to find.

The Preparatory Commission had already moved to Belgrave Square when I arrived, and Sir Alfred Zimmern had resigned because of his health, although he remained as a part-time adviser. Selected to succeed him as head of the Secretariat was Julian Huxley, the grandson of the famous Thomas Huxley and the brother of Aldous Huxley. One of Julian Huxley's deputies was my former professor and friend, Howard Wilson.

When I reached London, the staff was still small. During the day we read everything we could find on international organizations and international education (or science or culture, depending upon our role in the Secretariat). We talked with people who seemed to have ideas and we wrote to others. Often several of us had dinner together and talked far into the night. Then I would trudge home and put a shilling in the burner in my tiny bedroom to get a little heat in my damp quarters and try to sleep.

Within a few weeks our Education Division was a grand group of nine persons. It was headed by Dr. Kuo You-shou, who had been Minister of Education in Szechwan Province in China, and included men and women from Brazil, Denmark, France, Haiti, Mexico and the United States.

Dr. Wilson spent much time with us, and Joseph Lauwerys of the Institute of Education of the University of London and Pierre Rosello of the Bureau of Education in Geneva helped us as advisers.

Occasionally Dr. Huxley would join us, always adding new dimensions to our thinking. He was a world-famous biologist and zoologist, but he was at home in almost any subject. He was especially fond of the idea of pilot projects, likening them to the tiny boats which test the water to see if it is safe for the big boats to come to shore.

So we poked our heads into the clouds and then tested whether our feet would reach the ground, combining idealism with realism.

We worked hard, but we also had fun. Often Dr. Kuo would treat us to a sumptuous Chinese dinner, constantly filling our tea cups throughout the meal. After one of those repasts, someone suggested that we organize a Culinary Commission to travel around the world, testing whether the food of various nations contributed to international understanding or misunderstanding. Dr. Wilson suggested that a Chinese person be made chairman, but Dr. Kuo demurred. "It must be a Frenchman," he said, smiling. So we decided to make the Chinese and the French co-chairmen. Then someone asked what we should do with the British. "Make them a Trustee Territory," was the immediate rejoinder.

In 1946 the governments of the war-torn countries were in need of help immediately, rather than months later when UNESCO would be firmly established. So the Greek government presented UNESCO with a check for $5000 to be used in educational reconstruction, hoping by that gesture to prod other nations into more generous support for education in the war-devastated areas.

It was a small sum but a significant symbol. After much discussion, it was decided to use it for an educational mission to Greece. Dr. Huxley and Dr. Wilson asked me to undertake such a mission and they invited Dr. Harold Snyder of the Commission for International Educational Reconstruction of the American Council on Education to go, too.

My special assignment was to talk with teachers about their day-to-day problems. Consequently several groups of classroom teachers were assembled and I talked with them through an interpreter. Soon I had a list of 25 of their most pressing problems. Many of them dealt with the shattering experiences children had had during the war, and its aftermath. For example:

> Our children are restless, nervous, irritable. How can
> we help them to overcome these difficulties.
> Some of our children will not play at recess time or even
> leave the room for recess. What should we do?
> Some of our children take pleasure in destruction. How
> can we cope with this situation?

Such questions demanded an understanding of the psychology of the "post-war child" and I turned to the psychologists in the famed Tavistock Clinic in London: to Anna Freud; to Marie Paneth, who had worked with children from the German concentration camps; and to

110

others. On questions of health, I called upon the doctors in the United Nations Relief and Reconstruction Administration. In a similar way I consulted scores of experts.

Within a few weeks I was able to complete an illustrated booklet on *The Teacher and the Post-War Child in War-Devastated Countries,* which was published originally in English and French, and then in other languages. Sections of it were also printed in educational journals in several nations.

There was some flak from a few governmental representatives who claimed that there was no such human being as a "post-war child." Children are children, they maintained. How little they understood how everyday experiences shape and warp the minds as well as the bodies of boys and girls!

Once that booklet was completed, I began work on a smaller pamphlet, written at the request of Harold Snyder, to help raise funds in the United States for relief work. It was called *Going to School in War-Devastated Countries.* In it I told the story of schools in Norway during the German occupation, when children learned to overturn trains and carry on sabotage; gave an account of the "underground schools" in Poland during the Nazi period; depicted the heroic trek of thousands of students across China, carrying their "schools" on their backs; and narrated the story of schools in Greece. Thousands of copies of that booklet helped to raise large sums of money for the schools in war-torn nations.

Surely that $5000 was well used. It had multiplied like the loaves and fishes in the Bible. And, as Dr. Huxley pointed out, our trip to Greece had been UNESCO's first educational mission and these two booklets its first educational publications.

Shortly thereafter, J.P. Stephenson wrote a pamphlet on *Suggestions for Science Teachers in Devastated Countries.* That booklet was expanded later and eventually became UNESCO's best selling publication.

Meanwhile other members of the Secretariat were busy with plans for UNESCO's ongoing program. Slowly and sometimes painfully the total program took shape and by the fall of 1946 it was ready for the First General Conference of UNESCO.

In addition to our other work, we had to prepare for the move to Paris, where UNESCO was to have its permanent headquarters. Late in the spring of 1946 we moved there, where we were ensconced in the Hotel Majestic, near the Arc de Triomphe. During the German occupation of France, the Majestic had been the headquarters of the Gestapo. How appropriate for it now to be the headquarters of an international organization dedicated to peace and security.

UNESCO Underway

The United Nations Educational, Scientific, and Cultural Organization was launched with impressive ceremonies in the Grant Amphitheater of the College of the Sorbonne at the University of Paris on November 19, 1946. Then the delegates from the 28 Member States adjourned to UNESCO House to deliberate for three weeks on the program, the budget, the administration, and the personnel of this new, specialized agency.

The results of those three weeks included the appointment of Julian Huxley as Director General for a two-year term, the selection of an Executive Committee of 18 men, the tentative acceptance of an ambitious program, and the drawing up of a budget of a little less than seven million dollars, nearly a million of which was set aside to defray the expenses of the Preparatory Commission.

Nearly 150 projects had been approved, an unrealistic number for the Secretariat to handle. Four were eventually designated as top-priority topics: Reconstruction and Rehabilitation, Fundamental Education, the Hylean-Amazon Commission, and Education for International Understanding. Each of them represented the interests of strong forces at the conference.

The First General Conference had accomplished much, but it had been hurried and hectic, with the program tentatively approved before the budget had been submitted. Consequently the program plans were far more ambitious than the funds allocated for their implementation.

After the delegates departed, UNESCO House was a little like a home after a big party. There was lots of cleaning up to do. Those of us on the Secretariat had to rewrite the program in the light of the smaller budget, to draft administrative regulations, to draw up and circularize job descriptions for the posts in the permanent Secretariat, as well as launching a few programs.

It was then that I learned the importance of priorities, a valuable lesson for the rest of my life. We had enough projects in the Education Department to keep 50 persons busy, whereas our staff consisted of a dozen or so persons, few of whom were highly proficient in either French or English (the working languages of the organization).

Fortunately we did know that four projects were to be highlighted in the overall plan for UNESCO, two of them in the Education Department. Brief descriptions of the first three projects and a longer description of the fourth follow.

In the months after the Paris conference, the Reconstruction and Rehabilitation section moved along rapidly under the dedicated and dynamic leadership of Bernard Drzewieski, a small, stocky Pole who reminded some of us of Fiorella LaGuardia, and whom we referred to as "Dry Whiskey" because of our difficulty in pronouncing his name. Information was collected on the educational, scientific and cultural needs in war-devastated nations and hundreds of organizations alerted to the ways in which they could help. Thousands of books and other materials were provided and hundreds of scholarships awarded for study abroad. In addition, work camps in war-torn nations were assisted by UNESCO and the international work camp movement encouraged, a program in which I was especially interested.

Even in the 1940 s a few world leaders were concerned about the population explosion and the problem of food and people. Dr. Huxley was one of these. Rebuffed in his early attempts to work on family planning as a solution, he turned to the more acceptable program of providing more food for the world's people. One way to accomplish that was to help make the deserts bloom. Consequently he developed an ambitious and imaginative project to use the arid zones. He was likewise interested in the possibilities of the vast Hylean-Amazon area which he estimated could provide living space for 800 million people and produce enormous quantities of food for the people on our planet. That project did not achieve the success then that Huxley hoped it would, but the idea did catch on later.

In many parts of the world individuals, religious groups, special organizations, and governments had developed a variety of ways to promote literacy among adults and to find ways of encouraging people to help themselves in improving life in their villages or areas. That included such ideas as increasing and/or improving the local water supply, building feeder roads to main highways, and improving health conditions locally.

Because such work was considered important by several Member States of UNESCO, we asked 15 of the world's leaders in that work to write accounts of their experiences for UNESCO's first book — *Fundamental Education: Common Ground for All People.* In the early stages of that volume, I was in charge of the project. Then I had to turn it over to someone else because of the pressure of other duties.

In addition, several meetings were held at UNESCO House to decide on the best ways to tackle this far-flung program with the limited funds available. John Bowers of England, who had worked in fundamental education in Africa, was brought to Paris to head this work and a small staff was recruited to help him. Adopting the idea of pilot projects, UNESCO entered into an agreement with the government of Haiti to carry on a project in the Marbial Valley where illiteracy was certainly as high as 80% and where other problems plagued the people. That project, the first of many UNESCO programs in fundamental education, was launched in cooperation with the World

Health Organization and the Food and Agricultural Organization.

EDUCATION FOR INTERNATIONAL UNDERSTANDING

From the beginning of UNESCO many persons agreed that one of its major objectives should be to promote a climate of opinion throughout the world which would help to avert wars, to strengthen peace, and to enhance justice and freedom. It was agreed that all sections of the Secretariat would be charged with this responsibility, but that the Mass Communications, Social Science and Education sections should give high priority to this goal.

When the Education Department was reorganized after the First General Conference, I was designated as director of the education for international understanding division. Soon two able colleagues were recruited: Monica Luffman, who had been the executive secretary of the Council for Education for World Citizenship (in London), and Sheila Kidd. We were aided tremendously by our secretary, Marga Ovenstone, and from time to time by a trilingual secretary, Lucienne Hanni, from France. For the next two years that was the entire staff for a program which had been designated as one of the four top priority projects of UNESCO.

At the First General Conference there had been criticism of the term "education for international understanding," so we started a search for a better title. Some people wanted the word "world" included, such as education for world-mindedness, education for world community, or even education for world citizenship. But some people shied away from such terms as reflecting the idea of One World or world government. Others decried the term "world-mindedness" because it seemed to exclude the emotional aspects of learning.

A few liked the phrase "education for international cooperation," and I would have preferred that designation because it concentrated on action rather than knowledge. But that phrase was too advanced for many people.

Eventually we decided to retain the term "education for

international understanding" as the least objectionable phrase we could find. Years later I began to use the term "the international dimension of education" as best representing my point of view.

The time and energy expended on what may seem like a minor problem of semantics may seem ill-spent to some readers. Perhaps it was. But what we were really discussing was the philosophy reflected in such terminology — and that was extremely important.

In an effort to clarify the phrase, "education for international understanding," I wrote a brief statement for the Second General Conference in Mexico City in 1947. Here is a part of that statement:

> . . .begins by developing in children a sense of security and well-being, and attitudes of respect for individuals regardless of color, creed, race, or nationality.
>
> . . .involves the development of loyalty to the local community and the nation, and the extension of one's loyalty to the world. Such education requires an increase in and a refinement of national patriotism rather than a replacement of such patriotism by world loyalty. Nationalism and internationalism can be complementary loyalties.
>
> . . .includes a knowledge of and an appreciation for other lands and their peoples, and of the contributions of people of all races, religions, and nations to world culture.
>
> . . .incorporates a history of international conflicts and their causes, but stresses the interdependence of the modern world, the development of international cooperation, and the need for world community.
>
> . . .involves some study of the United Nations and its agencies.
>
> . . .includes a study of some of the most pertinent current events and contemporary problems.
>
> . . .stresses the development of the powers of critical thinking.
>
> . . .depends upon emotional as well as intellectual growth.
>
> . . .demands increasing opportunities for the development in pupils of responsibility through participation in school and community activities.
>
> . . .varies from nation to nation in the methods and materials employed, but emphasizes the same basic aims in all countries.
>
> . . .is a continuous and cumulative process and should be a major goal of education at all age levels.
>
> . . .is the task of other agencies of society, as well as schools.

116

. . .to be effective must use the accumulated knowledge of psychological and pedagogical research.

. . .should use the many media of communication and learning, including films, filmstrips, radio, recordings, etc.

Many people contributed to that charter of education for international understanding, but the final draft was mine. If I were to rewrite it today, I would make some changes in it, but it was advanced enough then to be provocative and yet not so radical as to lose us supporters.

Dr. Wilson and I were both convinced that the workshop way of learning was a giant step forward in educational methodology and we wanted to introduce it on a world-wide scale. What better way than to hold a series of workshops to explore various aspects of education for international understanding? So we wrote into the proposals for UNESCO's program plans for:

A seminar on education for international understanding for teachers of Member States, together with regional seminars along the same lines, if considered feasible by the Secretariat.

Obviously there was not time, personnel or money for regional seminars in 1947 so they were deleted in our rewrite of the program. We were satisfied with having introduced the idea of regional workshops; the idea could be implemented in the future.

Even the decision to hold one seminar was made with trepidation as the time to mount such a conference was distressingly short. Nevertheless we decided to convene such a meeting in Sevres, just outside Paris, in the summer of 1947. That location would permit us to draw upon the facilities and personnel of UNESCO and of Paris and would greatly facilitate our planning.

Dr. Wilson had left UNESCO but was persuaded to serve as director of this first international workshop. His expertise in running such seminars, his boundless energy, his intimate knowledge of UNESCO, and his background as an educator contributed immeasurably to the success of that venture.

There were several distinguished speakers, including Leon Blum, Julian Huxley, and Margaret Mead, and the

117

group leaders were outstanding. But Dr. Wilson and I were astounded that one of our workshop staff members, Hilda Taba, proved too bright, too quick, too perceptive, and too much the emancipated American woman for some of our participants. What a learning experience that was for us in cultural differences.

Of course there were problems. A few delegates were still suffering from the shock of the war and we did not allow enough time for them to vent their feelings early in the workshop. Some of the older delegates had taught about the League of Nations and were disillusioned about such teaching. Some delegates expected to sit and listen to lectures and were perturbed that they were expected to participate and produce documents. And several of the participants were very much aware of their professional status back home and refused for several days to become human beings. And there were language difficulties.

Even such seemingly unimportant details as the time for meals created problems. The Americans wanted to eat at 6 o'clock. The English said that 7 was plenty early. The French maintained that 8 was a much more civilized hour to dine. And the Latin Americans were shocked that anyone would eat before 9. Since we were in France, we ate at 8 and the Americans learned the importance of celebrating "high tea" in the English fashion.

Despite difficulties the workshop gathered momentum, and by the end of six weeks almost all of the 82 participants from 31 nations agreed that they had had a unique, stimulating, and profitable experience in international living and learning. In addition, we had proved that the workshop way of learning could be applied internationally.

During the summer of 1947 UNESCO conducted three workshops. One was on teacher education and was held in England, directed by Karl Bigelow of the U.S.A. Another, on childhood education, was held in Czechoslovakia, with Asa Skaard of Norway as the director. The third was on Education for a World Society: Teaching About the United Nations and Its Specialized Agencies. It was held at Adelphi College on Long Island, near enough for the participants to visit the U.N. frequently and to draw upon the staff and facilities of the U.N. and many other organizations in New York City, yet far enough removed from that exciting metropolis to avoid its attractions and distractions.

Dr. Y.R. Chao of China was the director but the major responsibility for the workshop was mine. I made all the preliminary arrangements, served as executive secretary and behind-the-scenes manager, and chaired one of the study groups.

I was determined to get that workshop rolling quickly. So we started on a Wednesday evening, taking Thursday and Friday to get acquainted and to let people tell about their experiences during World War II, and about education in their countries. On Saturday we bounced the delegates around Manhattan in a bus, treated them to lunch in an Automat, and took them to a concert at the Lewissohn Stadium that evening. On Sunday we took them to Jones Beach for a swim. By Monday they were human beings rather than educational dignitaries, and the major business of the seminar could start.

In their six weeks together the participants listened to many distinguished lecturers, visited the U.N. several times, viewed many films and filmstrips, and did a great deal of reading. Each of the 50 delegates from 23 nations worked individually with a staff member on a writing project for use back home. In addition, we arranged for the participants to meet Dwight Eisenhower at Columbia University and Eleanor Roosevelt at Val Kil.

Several of our documents were published by UNESCO and many of the projects of the delegates were published by their governments, so there was a tremendous outreach from this six weeks' seminar.

Another project on which our Education for International Understanding division worked was the production of *A Handbook for the Improvement of Textbooks and Other Teaching Materials as Aids to International Understanding.* That publication was edited by I. James Quillen of Stanford University and drew heavily upon the experience of the Scandinavian countries in exchanging the manuscripts of accounts of their countries with each other for comments, and upon the studies made in the U.S.A. of teaching materials on Asia, Latin America and Canada.

Monica Luffman also produced a booklet on *International Relations Clubs and Similar Societies* which proved useful in many places in the formation of UNESCO Clubs and similar groups.

A project which took less time than others and was the most fun was the preparation of a picture book for children which I put together, called *Let's Visit Unesco House*. It was published originally in French and English, and later in other languages.

In order to involve educators in the Member States of UNESCO in an examination of the international dimension of their educational institutions, we suggested that each country submit a report every two years on eight aspects of their system. Those eight parts were to be on 1) teaching about the U.N. and its related agencies, 2) teaching about other lands and peoples, 3) teaching about human beings and group relations, 4) teaching about international interdependence, international conflict, international cooperation, and the need for world community, 5) teaching about current events and contemporary problems, 6) developing critical thinking, 7) broadening the experiences of students in democratic citizenship, and 8) educating teachers for international understanding. Questions were included for each of those topics.

That proposal was overly ambitious and the General Conference settled for reports only on the first point. But there is much merit in the general design suggested for this survey and I still hope that someday UNESCO Member States will decide to report on some of the other points in this eight-pronged program, other than merely the first section.

Leaving UNESCO

When anyone goes abroad to work, he usually needs to

bear in mind two possibilities. One is to stay for life or a long term of service, with the risk of losing contacts back home and of finding it difficult to find employment upon his return. The other is to stay for only a short time, to make whatever contribution he can make and learn whatever he can, returning then to his native land.

The work at UNESCO had been exciting and the opportunities for service great. Nevertheless I decided to return to the United States to study. At that time I asked three men in the Secretariat to write recommendations for me. Each of them did so and each of them gave me a copy of his statement, a practice which is usually frowned upon. I hope it is not too immodest to end this chapter with excerpts from those recommendations.

Dr. Huxley, an Englishman, wrote about his regret that I had decided to leave, and went on to say:

> You have worked hard and successfully for UNESCO and I am sure that what you have built up represents an asset of permanent value to the Organization. I am very glad that your time with UNESCO ends with the extremely successful Seminar at Adelphi College where your skill and devotion were appreciated by many outside observers as well as by ourselves in UNESCO.

Dr. Laves, the Deputy Director General and an American, wrote about the premium placed on people with adaptability in the early stages of a new organization, praising me for that quality and the wide range of projects in which I had participated. Then he ended with this comment:

> If I might summarize my impressions. . .it would be that first of all he brought to his work high professional competence, and secondly, that he brought an attitude of humility and understanding that made him almost the ideal type of international civil servant.

Dr. Beebe, the Assistant Director General for Education, and a New Zealander, wrote:

> During his time here he has made a valuable contribution not only to the Education Department but to UNESCO as a whole. . . UNESCO was particularly fortunate in having in Dr. Kenworthy an educator whose international outlook enabled him to use his knowledge of the American classroom to help teachers in other

parts of the world. He was an excellent team-worker. . . .The part he played in the Seminar at Adelphi College in 1948 was particularly notable and his dependability and willingness to work hard, were then, as throughout his career, of immense value.

I left UNESCO in the fall of 1948 with gratitude to the people I had met and with whom I had worked and for the incredible experience of taking part in the creation of the world's first significant international educational organization.

CHAPTER 9

Working on My Doctoral Degree and Taking Part in a Survey of Education in Puerto Rico

My work in UNESCO had been exciting and rewarding, with a wide range of responsibilities and some influence. In a sense a sizeable portion of the world had been my classroom. After such an experience, it was difficult to think of returning to a single classroom or even a single school in the U.S.A.

I wanted now to have time for research, reading and reflection, exploring as deeply as possible the ways in which people form attitudes and how attitudes can be reinforced or changed. Just where that would lead vocationally, I was not sure. It might mean work with future teachers, curriculum work in a school system, or a position with some out-of-school agency in world affairs. At that moment I was not unduly concerned about a job.

Long ago I had realized that doctoral work ought to be done with an expert in one's field, and, if possible, with a person whom one could admire as a human being. At the Second General Conference of UNESCO in Mexico City, I had met such a man. He was Donald Tewksbury. He had been raised in China and had absorbed much of the best of that culture. He was an authority in international education, with a strong interest in UNESCO. And he was a wonderful human being.

So I bade my colleagues at UNESCO House goodbye

123

and set off for New York City in the fall of 1948 to study at Teachers College, Columbia University.

I considered taking my doctorate in social studies, but finally decided to take it in Curriculum and Teaching, with a strong emphasis upon comparative and international education. When I talked with my adviser, I indicated that I wanted to take several courses in anthropology and in social psychology. But the requirements for my degree ruled out such courses and I had to resort to "sneaking" such work into my reading for other courses.

I found a room at International House on Riverside Drive and settled in there for an intensive year of work, hoping to complete my work in that period of time. "I House," as it was affectionately known by most residents, was a fascinating place, with half the students from abroad and half from the U.S.A. There was a wide range of activities and one could obtain a good education by participating in many of them. But I had decided to obtain a degree and so I passed up many opportunities in that interesting institution. I did, however, meet many students from abroad informally, learning much from them.

I also decided not to try to find a job as I had done while working on my master's degree. This time I had enough savings to get me through a year of graduate studies and I was determined not to dissipate my energies or risk my health again by working.

My Courses at Teachers College

Some of my courses were disappointing, but there were some which were most gratifying. For example, I took two courses with Professor Florence Stratemeyer, who was one of the most thorough and widely read people I had ever met in the curriculum field. From her I learned much, especially about her theory of "persistent life situations" as the basis for curricula, ideas which were eventually included in her volume on *Developing a Curriculum for Modern Living*. And she was a gracious, generous and charming woman.

With Alice Miel I took courses in Social Learnings and in Supervision. She was particularly adept at using group processes without becoming enslaved by them. And she was "tops" in role playing. I felt fortunate to become her graduate assistant and in later years to teach her course in Social Learnings when she was on leave from T.C. Above all I was impressed with her keen interest in all her students, even in large classes.

There were also interesting courses with Roma Gans, Gordon MacKenzie, and others.

It was my work with Professor Tewksbury, however, which stands out in bas relief. He was a remarkable man, with tremendous scholarship, a desire to try out new ideas in teaching, a warm human sympathy, and a prescient view of world affairs. He had just completed a seven-year reading program, reading for a year or so on each of the social science disciplines to see what he could learn about their contribution to international education. He was trying to apply to his teaching the insights he had gained from this reading.

Consequently some of his class sessions were thrilling. Others were "duds." But he was willing to try out new ideas, even if they failed. For example, he almost always played some appropriate music as we entered the class, thereby setting the tone for the lectures, panels or discussions. And after every session, we were all required to write short "reaction papers" which were returned to us with comments, but no grades.

Occasionally he used outside speakers as resource persons and he often had panels of students from abroad as a part of a session. He was also a master in the art of questioning. Occasionally he hurt a student, but most of the time he used his "rapier" with finesse. He believed that the attitudes of many graduate students could be changed only by a kind of shock treatment and he used that method often and usually successfully.

I also spent hours in his office discussing world affairs, UNESCO, teaching methods, and other topics, emerging from those sessions stimulated by this contact.

Unfortunately Dr. Tewksbury took a semester's leave during my second semester to work in the Hoover Library in California. But he had already discussed my doctoral dissertation with me and I had begun work on it before he left. From then on we corresponded and his suggestions were enormously helpful.

I had expected to be working at T.C. with a group of doctoral candidates who would help each other through this difficult educational and emotional experience. I was stunned to discover, instead, the most competitive group with whom I had ever worked or studied. Most of them were extraordinary as individuals but several of them were extremely aggressive, especially in our doctoral seminar. Anyway, we lived through "300 CR," as that course was called, but I shall remember it with consternation until the end of my life.

Working on My Doctoral Dissertation

For my dissertation I was clear that I wanted to work on the international dimension of education, from kindergarten through teacher education (pre-service and in-service). Some of that interest stemmed from my year in Germany and some of it from my work with UNESCO. Much of it came from the reading of a study by Otto Klineberg on *Tensions Affecting International Understanding: A Survey of Research,* a seminal volume in international education.

Of course the topic was too big for a dissertation. In fact it was large enough for three or four such projects. Eventually I wrote three books and a sizeable pamphlet from my original dissertation outline. They were *Introducing Children to the World: In Elementary and Junior High Schools; International Understanding Through the Secondary School Curriculum; World Horizons for Teachers;* and *The International Dimension of Education.* So I decided to concentrate on the education of teachers for my dissertation, believing that little could be done with students unless their teachers were internationally-minded.

126

The research and the writing was hard work, but it was fun, too. It brought together many of my experiences, reading and thinking of the past few years, like a giant jigsaw puzzle.

When it was completed, it was submitted to the members of my dissertation committee in the usual "hearing" or "examination." Fortunately that was not the traumatic experience for me that it is for some people. The members of my committee commended me for the document and recommended to the Teachers College Press that it be published in a series of books called "Studies in Education." It appeared with some cutting and polishing, in 1952, with the title *World Horizons for Teachers*. It had a brisk but limited sale and some influence, I think. Perhaps the most valuable part of it was "A Check List of Activities for Developing World-Minded Teachers," which I devised. That list was divided into sections for pre-service education and for in-service education.

LEARNING ABOUT EDUCATION IN PUERTO RICO

Almost as soon as I had enrolled at Teachers College, I was asked if I would be interested in going to Puerto Rico as a graduate assistant in the survey of that island being conducted by the Institute of Field Studies of Teachers College.

I was tempted to say "Yes" immediately. Then I remembered that I had returned to the United States to get a degree — the "union card" for many jobs. Wouldn't this be an interruption of that work? The professors in charge of the survey said it would not be. In fact, several of them with whom I would be taking courses would be on the survey. So I accepted and spent a few weeks in Puerto Rico that fall.

Five of us were invited to become research assistants. Four of us were Helen Borland, Verna Dieckman, Charles Dorrance and I. The fifth was Lawrence Cremin, who became a regular member of the team when John Ivey, Jr., was not able to come to Puerto Rico. Since that time

Larry has become well-known as a brilliant writer on the history of American education and more recently as President of Teachers College.

The Survey Team was composed of a large number of distinguished professors from T.C. Among those from the curriculum and teaching division were Professors Cunningham, Fields, Lawler, MacKenzie, Miel, and Stratemeyer.

And how we worked! We were up early and to bed late. In between we visited schools, conferred with government officials, read documents, and wrote. But we played, too. We had a leisurely dinner almost every evening, listening to the hypnotic Latin rhythms of the hotel orchestra and dancing to it. A couple of times we went swimming despite the warning of the hotel people about the heavy undertow of the water. But after dinner and the dancing, we worked as a group, reviewing the day's work and planning the next steps.

My part in this venture was small but interesting. I was asked to work on the social studies curriculum for Puerto Rican schools and to ascertain how the cultural heritage of the Island could be incorporated into the curriculum, especially in music and art.

Probably the most difficult decision for the team to make was on language instruction. Since the turn of the century, English had theoretically been used as the language of instruction in the schools. Should this be continued or should Spanish be used? My experience with UNESCO was helpful at this point and I could emphasize the fact that in every part of the world the language of instruction in the early grades was the language children heard at home. Fortunately this was the point of view of the bilingual specialist on the team, Virginia French. In the final report it was recommended that Spanish be the basis of instruction in the early grades, but that English be introduced very early as a second language. The use of the Island radio and of English-speaking persons from the Mainland was urged to make the teaching of English effective.

Because I was only a graduate assistant, I waited a

long time before raising a question which had been on my mind. Then I decided to air it, asking whether our report really took into consideration the unique background of the Island, with its mixture of cultures. Several members of the team agreed with this comment, and eventually Alice Miel was asked to assume responsibility for making sure that the document included this point of view and was not written as a proposal that could be used in any state of the U.S.A.

It was interesting and sometimes frustrating to see a group of educators from the Mainland adjust to a new culture. Most of them did so very well but others had their difficulties. I recall, for example, the frustration of one of them who was an expert on child and adolescent psychology and was amazed to find no major "disciplinary situations" in the schools. Because of a different cultural pattern, many of her "yardsticks" of child and adolescent behavior had to be abandoned and new ones developed.

The results of many months of work by the Teachers College team were reported in a volume on *Public Education and The Future of Puerto Rico,* published in 1950.

Completing Work on the Doctorate

Despite this "interruption," I was able to complete the course work at T.C. in the summer of 1949. Meanwhile I had studied for the written exam with two friends — Donald Bruner, who has spent his life as an outstanding elementary school principal in Portland, Oregon, and Charles Dorrance, who has distinguished himself as a professor of education at the University of Florida.

I was invited to membership in the two honorary educational fraternities and decided to accept only one invitation, to Kappa Delta Phi.

Soon I had completed the courses, passed all the exams, and completed my dissertation. Eventually I received the degree of Doctor of Education and could now write, Leonard S. Kenworthy, A.B.; M.A.; Ed. D. For a while it was gratifying to be called Dr. Kenworthy, but the novelty soon wore off and I was glad to be known as Leonard, Ken, or Mr. Kenworthy.

CHAPTER 10

College Teaching and Two Nationally Significant Attempts To Improve Teacher Education

With my doctoral degree in sight, I started a search for a job in the spring of 1949. There were several offers but I finally narrowed them down to two. One was the job of social studies coordinator for the school system of Brookline, Massachusetts. The other was a professorship at Brooklyn College.

I spent three days in Brookline, a wealthy suburb of Boston with an outstanding school system, and was impressed with several of the people I met and much that I saw. But I hesitated to accept a job there because so many of the social studies teachers were older people who did not seem interested in changes. As I boarded the train for New York, the superintendent of schools asked me why I didn't accept his offer and save us both correspondence. I replied that I was still considering another attractive offer. Then he said, "But no one ever turns down a chance to come to Brookline." That statement confirmed my impression of smugness and the die was cast. It would be Brooklyn College.

That same week Carleton Washburne, the chairman of the Education Department and the Dean of Teacher Education of Brooklyn College, entertained me in his apartment overlooking Central Park. He and his wife and I had a wonderful dinner and stimulating conversation as we roamed the world together. But there was no confirmation of the job. An hour passed. Two hours. Three hours. Finally Heluiz Washburne placed her hand on her husband's arm and said, "Why don't you tell him he's hired, Carleton?" To which he replied, "He knows that, dear," adding, "Don't you, Leonard?" I assured him that I had thought so but had begun to wonder.

In the coming years I learned how typical that exchange was. Heluiz Washburne was a wise and wonderful woman — bright, attractive, a gracious hostess, an eminent writer of children's books, and a warm and understanding human being.

The job at Brooklyn College appealed to me for several reasons. Most of my life I had been associated with independent schools, despite the fact that I had attended public schools in the elementary and junior high school grades. This position would give me an opportunity to become associated with the largest public school system in the United States, with nearly 50,000 teachers and nearly a million students.

That job would also give me a chance to teach courses in the social studies, which I was eager to do.

Furthermore, it would bring me into close contact with one of the world's leading educators. As noted earlier, Washburne had made the Winnetka, Illinois, system world-famous. He was a progressive educator but a sane one who believed in rigorous standards of research. In addition, he was a pioneer and hoped to embark on new programs in teacher education and in international education.

Finally, New York City seemed to me an exciting place in which to live and not just a fascinating place to visit.

So I accepted the offer of a job in the Education Department of Brooklyn College, with the understanding that I would become an Associate Professor as soon as I received my doctorate.

BROOKLYN COLLEGE

In those days Brooklyn College was well on its way to

becoming a nationally famous institution. Founded in 1926, it was one of the four colleges (later 20 colleges) of the City University of New York.

Its buildings were red brick and Georgian in style. The grounds had been landscaped by the City Parks Commission and were maintained by them as a public park. The style of architecture and the arrangement of the buildings struck me as symbolic — an attempt to reproduce in a city college the atmosphere of an Ivy League institution.

In its earliest years Brooklyn College had suffered from political influence. But when Harry Gideonse became President, things began to change. He was a brilliant economist, a champion of liberal arts education, and a strong administrator. In his first few months on the campus, he clashed with the communist and other left-wing students and there were some bitter battles. Sometimes Gideonse resorted to ruthless tactics. But he was determined to win and finally did. Meanwhile he assembled an outstanding faculty and established the college as a nationally-known institution of the first rank.

As a newcomer I was impressed with the size of the faculty. At my first faculty meeting, we filled an auditorium which seated 900 persons. In addition, there were many part-time people who taught in the Graduate Division and in the School of General Studies. I was also impressed with the caliber of the professors.

I was also struck with the students. Many of them were bright and eager to learn. Admission at that time depended upon an 87 average in the city high schools. Of course it paid to work for such an average as it guaranteed a free college education.

Many of the students were diamonds in the rough, socially and culturally. As the sons and daughters of first- or second-generation immigrants, many spoke some language at home other than English. This could have been a great asset to them and to the United States, but they were often ashamed of it and eventually lost their ability to function in two languages.

A high percentage of our students and faculty were

Jewish. But many of them were in revolt against their religious background and were culturally but not religiously Jewish. Nevertheless, the high regard in which Jews have always held learning was a tremendous plus factor at Brooklyn College.

Altogether the student body in the late 40s included something over 20,000 students, with more than half of them taking courses in the late afternoons and evenings. Later there were over 30,000.

THE EDUCATION DEPARTMENT OF BROOKLYN COLLEGE

As chairman of the Education Department and Dean of Teacher Education, Dr. Washburne had inherited a very good faculty. On it were several people who were nationally known and respected. For example, Lester and Alice Crow were the authors of several college texts in education; Lester Dix had been the principal of the famous Horace Mann-Lincoln School at Teachers College; and Gertrude Hildreth had been the psychologist in the Horace Mann-Lincoln School.

State funds were now available for a fifth-year program in teacher education at Brooklyn College and a large number of new positions were therefore open. With characteristic zeal, he began to build an outstanding faculty, utilizing his many contacts at home and abroad to fill those posts.

Because all of the students and most of the faculty at Brooklyn College were from New York City, Washburne felt the college tended to be provincial rather than cosmopolitan. The only way he could see to change this situation was to hire professors from other parts of the United States and the world. In the next few years he persuaded several persons who had been born abroad or who had worked many years abroad, to come to Brooklyn. They included Alfred Adler from Austria; Lenore Boehm, a German who had studied with Jean Piaget in Switzerland; Margaret Cormack, who had lived much of her life in India; Brenda Lansdowne, an English educator; and Eunice Matthew, who had just completed a period of several years for UNESCO in Thailand. In addition, he hired several of us who came from other parts of the United States, including several Negroes.

However, we did not realize that in coming to Brooklyn College we were entering a hornet's nest. In his first year on campus, Washburne had dismissed several people who were almost ready for life tenure in order to fill those positions with people he had selected. Some of us were also brought in at relatively high ranks. When he appointed professors from outside New York City, a few interpreted this as anti-Semitism. To add coals to the fire, he had unfortunately said publicly that he had brought in the newcomers to show the old-timers how to teach. The fact that he held the purse strings of the new state funds for teacher education also gave him tremendous power. In addition, he was a well-known progressive educator at a time when such ideas were not popular on college campuses.

As a result of these and other factors, there was considerable criticism of Washburne and of the new members of our department, who were caricatured as The Western Tornado.

PLANNING A NEW TEACHER EDUCATION PROGRAM

Washburne believed that the education program at Brooklyn College, as well as in other institutions, did not prepare students adequately for teaching. The courses were too verbal and the students had too little contact with children. Methods courses also concentrated upon specific subject fields rather than emphasizing the integration of knowledge. And the policy of starting the program with the history of education and the philosophy of education "turned off" many prospective teachers.

So we began a long-range study of ways to improve teacher education. In order to involve everyone in the department, he organized several small, self-selected study groups of from eight to ten persons each, known as Policy Groups. Each of them met weekly for a period of two years. Each group also selected one person to serve as its representative on a Framework Committee, the overall planning body for the department.

After a long and sometimes bitter struggle, a new teacher education program was adopted by a narrow vote. In it all students took a beginning course, known as Ed. 10, which was constructed around the questions which prospective teachers most frequently asked. It included some material on the growth and development of children and adolescents and some on the society in which they were being reared. Each student made an intensive study of a child or adolescent and the classes took several trips to schools and community agencies. In addition, the students observed the administering of tests and interviews in the Education Clinic through a one-way vision room and watched children in the Early Childhood Center on campus through a similar arrangement. Those two centers, both instituted by Washburne, were considered by many of us as valuable additions to the department.

In the second year (usually when students were juniors), they took two courses simultaneously, with the professors in those courses sometimes working closely together. One was a year-long course in Human Growth and Development. The other was on Education and Modern Society. Originally the students in those two courses included both prospective elementary and secondary school teachers. At the same time students worked for 45 hours a semester in some community agency in order to gain firsthand experience in working with boys and girls in an informal situation.

In their senior year all students took a two-semester program in methods. Simultaneously all prospective teachers observed one semester in the schools and then had a semester of student teaching. All the professors in the methods courses were responsible for supervising their students in the schools.

In the fifth year, or graduate program, all students were required to take a workshop in which the problems of their current teaching were tackled. Then they were given a choice of taking two out of three courses: the Philosophy

7)	Education for an Industrial Society: Japan.	Japanese educator to be interviewed in class; discussion.	Chapter in King book on Japan.
8)	Mid-term examination.	Open book exam.	
9)	The United Nations: An Overview.	Film *Overture* and discussion.	Coyle's paperback on the U.N.
10)	UNESCO: World Agency for Education.	Lecture and discussion.	Start work on term project-final exam.
11)	Teaching about the U.N. and Its Agencies in American Schools.	Lecture and discussion.	Work on paper.
12)	The International Dimension of Education in U.S. Schools: Aims.	Lecture and discussion.	Work on paper.
13)	The International Dimension of Education in U.S. Schools: Methods.	Lecture and discussion.	Work on paper.
14)	The International Dimension of Education in U.S. Schools: Materials.	Book exhibit.	Work on paper.
15)	Concluding Remarks and Unfinished Business.	Concluding remarks and class questions.	Term project – final exam due.

Three comments may be in order here to explain certain aspects of that course. The "general book" assignment was intended primarily to broaden the background of students on the world community. A long, annotated list was included in the syllabus, including such volumes as Boulding's *The Meaning of the Twentieth Century,* Cousins' *Who Speaks for Man?*, Kluckhohn's *Mirror for Man,* and Dean's *Nature of the Non-Western World.* The assignment was to write a reaction paper rather than a review of the book selected.

The combined term project-final exam was primarily on the international dimension of the student's own classroom. One section of it was the compiling of a list of materials, amounting to $100, which the student would like to purchase for use in his or her school. Over the years many students persuaded their schools to purchase those materials, which amounted to thousands of dollars worth of useable, new resources.

In the use of speakers, I learned after several disappointing experiences to interview such persons in front of the class rather than to have them lecture for an hour or so. In that way I could elicit the information I wanted the class to get, and as I posed questions, I could fill in any background which I thought the students needed.

Over the years two of the sessions became well known by my colleagues and several of them attended those meetings. One was the evening in which we role-played a conference of Russian educators; the other was the evening when I brought in 300 or so books for the students to examine in small groups for their $100 assignment.

One of the most gratifying results of the course was the fact that several students eventually went overseas to teach, often with the Peace Corps.

SOME CHANGES IN OUR NEW TEACHER EDUCATION PROGRAM

Following Dr. Washburne's retirement, Joseph Justman was elected chairman of the Education Department and appointed by President Gideonse as Dean of Teacher Education.

Professor Justman felt that after years of turmoil and tension, the Education Department needed a period of calm, so there were few innovations during his period as chairman. However, several changes were made in the program on which we had worked so long and hard. Ed. 20 was abolished and a course in curriculum added. The policy of requiring two semesters of observation and student teaching by prospective secondary school teachers was altered and only the practice teaching semester was retained. And the practice at both the elementary and secondary levels of having methods teachers supervise all their students in the schools was modified, with several persons hired specifically to supervise, even though they did not teach the methods courses.

Some people felt that those changes would strengthen

our program. Others were willing to go along with Professor Justman's modifications. Some of us felt that those changes seriously weakened our preparation of teachers.

About that time I began to think of leaving Brooklyn College. I was interviewed for several jobs and given some tempting offers, including the presidencies of a Quaker college, a teacher education institution in New England, and a Black College, as well as deanships of schools of education in New Jersey, New York and Pennsylvania. But they were all administrative jobs and I really didn't want to become an administrator, especially as I was so sensitive to criticism; I wanted to teach. So I decided to remain at Brooklyn College, a decision which still seems to have been a good one.

STRIKES, DISTURBANCES AND RIOTS

Throughout American history colleges have often been ivory towers or retreats from real life. That was not true, however, in the late 60s and early 70s when college campuses across the U.S.A. became battlegrounds in the civil rights war and in the protest movement against the fighting in Vietnam. In that period Brooklyn College had its share of the action.

In October 1968, the B.C. community was like a large cider jug which had been violently shaken and was ready to explode. Triggered by the presence of Navy Recruiting Officers in the lobby of the main building, many students and some faculty took part in protests which led to disturbances and a near riot. The police were called and that fanned the flames. Students careened through the corridors and classrooms, causing considerable damage to the buildings and some harm to individuals.

Soon the Faculty Council was summoned and in the next few days we spent hours examining the causes of the disturbances, listening to representatives of various groups, and working on changes in administration, curricular offerings, and extracurricular activities, in order to meet the just and unjust charges brought by students and faculty.

143

Those were tense times. On several occasions we were surrounded by students as we deliberated. At least twice the doors were blocked so that we could not leave. And at one historic session a small group of Black students accused college officials of running an institution for Jews. In protest, several of the Jews on the Faculty Council walked out of the meeting. But they returned in time for an upcoming crucial vote.

As one of the elected representatives, I took part in hours of discussion, although I was never an influential participant. I am proud, however, of the fact that when we were drafting the resolution that called for a large increase in the number of Black students, that my amendment to broaden the category to include students from "poverty areas" was accepted, thus including many Puerto Ricans, Americans of Chinese ancestry, and some whites with lower economic backgrounds.

Other changes which were instituted as a result of the disturbances included several I could support, such as student involvement in curriculum planning and student input regarding the teaching of professors. Some proposals, however, I could not support, such as student participation in the hiring and firing of faculty. Unfortunately the zeal of students subsided and many of them were remiss in attending committee meetings to which they had been appointed and in following through on other forms of student involvement they had won.

I was particularly pleased that a course on Education and the African Heritage was added to the graduate offerings in our department and that I was asked to teach that course with Professor Kerina of Southwest Africa. But I was disappointed in the enrollment as it drew only a dozen students, most of them white. Perhaps that course had been merely a symbol of protest. At the time of the protests against the war in Vietnam, the Education Department elected a small strategy committee on which I served.

Many of my students were highly critical of the Open Enrollment plan whereby Blacks and others were to enter the city colleges. Often they said directly or indirectly,

"We made it; why can't they?" In reply I often asked them:

> Was your religion ever destroyed?
> Was your family life destroyed?
> Was pride in your past destroyed?
> Have you been slaves in the last 300 years?
> Were you ever Black?

Those questions did not reflect any diminuation of my admiration for all that Jews have accomplished, but they were intended to point up the differences between the experiences of Jews and Blacks in the U.S.A.

A Second Attempt To Improve Teacher Education

Some of us had never been satisfied with our first attempt to improve teacher education at Brooklyn College. We were proud of the gains we had made in that program but felt that it had not gone far enough. And we felt that the alterations in it had hurt rather than helped it. By the late 60s it was certainly "dated."

Among those who felt that way was Louis Rosenzweig, then Chairman of the Department of Education. He and others emphasized the need for a new look at teacher education in the light of our experience with our previous program and of such changes around us as the decentralization of school administration in New York City; the hiring of para-professionals; the new insights in such fields as anthropology and urban sociology; the development of computer-assisted-instruction and other technological innovations; and the urgent need to relate the college more closely to the community.

From the combined concern of many of us came another intensive study of teacher education. Several small groups of faculty, known this time as "Target Groups," met scores of times and forwarded their findings to the Curriculum Committee of the department. Several ad hoc committees were formed and their conclusions fed into the overall plan.

The major responsibility for the new plan, however, was carried by members of the Curriculum Committee, chaired by Professor Natalie Darcy, an able educator who was extremely well acquainted with the department, with the college, and with Brooklyn. That committee deliberated for nearly three years. On it were Zita Cantwell, Sam Duker, Dorothy Geddes, Charles Long, Rose Mukerji, Bernard Starr, Elvira Tarr and myself. Celia Baum served as the liaison person with the Graduate Committee on Curriculum.

Scores of changes were proposed and many of them adopted. Two were of major importance. One was the decision to shift from an observation-based program to an experience-based plan. In every course students would have firsthand experiences, starting with a tutoring experience and proceeding to an interneship or apprentice position. The second major focus of our new plan was on the development of Teaching-Learning Centers near schools in several parts of Brooklyn. They were to serve somewhat as extension centers of the college. In them students would work with school children, and some of our college classes would be held there. Many, but not all of them, were to be in poverty areas so that future teachers could become conversant with the communities in which they would probably teach, rather than undergoing "culture shock" when they began their student teaching, as had happened so often in the past.

To carry out this ambitious and relevant approach, we envisioned "teams" of college professors which would be partially self-selected and include psychologists, social scientists and philosophers, as well as curriculum and methods experts.

In this new program there would be several "core seminars." But there would also be more electives than we had previously had, in order to provide more for individual needs and interests.

After years of work and scores of meetings, this plan was finally adopted in the spring of 1971. It had taken us 20 years, but at last we had a teacher education program based on firsthand experiences with children and adolescents.

Most of us realized that the success of this new program would depend upon many factors. One would be the availability of funds. Another would be the development of several well-located, well-housed, and well-equipped Teaching-Learning Centers. A third would be the success of the team teaching idea. And a fourth would be the size of classes. A factor with which we did not reckon was the drastic cutback of funds for the City University as a result of the financial crisis of New York City in 1975.

In formulating this new program I served as chairman of the Task Force on The Middle School, as a member of the Curriculum Committee, and for a short period as acting chairman of that group during a leave of absence of Dr. Darcy. I was also the only member of that planning committee who had served on the Framework Committee during the previous attempt to update the teacher education program at Brooklyn College.

Throughout all the years described in this chapter I was active in the roles mentioned here. But the major portion of my time, thought and energy was devoted to the education of future social studies teachers, including the supervision of their student teaching. That will be described in detail in the next chapter.

CHAPTER 11

Helping Future Social Studies Teachers

Courses in education, and especially in methods of teaching, should provide some of the most stimulating classes in colleges. Frequently they do. But much too often they are irrelevant and insipid.

My own experiences in education courses as an undergraduate may illustrate what I mean. Instead of helping us in our planning of lessons or assisting us in seeing our lessons in the broad framework of the purposes of the social studies, our methods professor at Earlham saddled us with a course in historiography. And in another education course we spent most of our time on schools in the American colonies, with little time left for schools and their purposes in the present. Perhaps such experiences were an incentive for me to become a professor of methods in the social studies and a supervisor of student teachers. Who knows?

In my methods courses at Brooklyn College I was determined to be practical and helpful. Almost as soon as they were seated on the first day of a course, I began to carry out that resolve. I told the students that I knew they wanted a practical course and that I would try to be down-to-earth in my approach. Since they were concerned with lesson planning, we would start immediately on that topic. I then asked them to jot down quickly their ideas or "aims" for the first session of our course.

149

Most of them were flabbergasted at this point as they had expected a lengthy lecture by the prof. But when they saw that I meant business, they went to work. When their lists were completed, we read them aloud and discussed them. Almost always their aims included the assignment of a text, the collection of "course cards," and some information about their student teaching — all clerical items.

"What *social* aims are included in your plans for today's class in the social studies?" I then asked. Inevitably that led to a discussion of the aims in a social studies methods course and eventually to a discussion of the ways in which a class could become a social unit. Often we used buzz groups to involve more students in the discussion. Then I usually gave a thumb-nail sketch of myself and asked the students to write brief autobiographies for the next class which I could use to become acquainted with them and eventually utilize to gain data for my written recommendations of them. I also told them that this would be the first entry in a cumulative folder about them, to which they would have access.

The mundane matters were usually taken care of by the end of the second session. Then we could turn to the central question of why one should teach the social studies to boys and girls. Since most of my students were history majors, their pat reply was to help students to understand the present. At that point I would ask them how students could ever understand the present if they spent years examining the past in chronological order and did not reach the present until they took a Problems of Democracy course in their senior year in high school.

Often these prospective teachers were jolted when I asked them if they used "the historical approach" to get acquainted with a new friend on a date, starting with their birth and then coming on down, year by year, to the present. Gradually most of them came to see that one could also start with the present, gradually fitting in pertinent information from the past which helps to explain the current scene. Thus we were off to a consideration of alternate approaches in the social studies, a theme we examined often.

In most of my classes we sat around tables, seminar style, even if we had to have two rows around the tables. And ordinarily I sat rather than stood. An informal physical environment does not guarantee informality, but it can help.

Gradually I shared with students some of my ideas on the meaning of the social studies and of social studies teaching, trying to remember that it takes time to budge people from their cherished views. Eventually I gave them copies of one such statement which has appeared in my methods books for elementary and for secondary school teachers, namely:

> To discover and develop the abilities of every person so that he or she may comprehend himself or herself and other human beings better, cope with life more effectively, contribute to society in his or her own ways, help improve society, enjoy it, and share in its benefits.

Obviously that is a broad statement, but so are the social studies. To me the phrase "social studies" is a kind of shorthand for the study of people. In reality this field should be called geography-anthropology-sociology-psychology-social psychology-economics-history-government, plus a few other hyphenated terms like music - art - linguistics - philosophy - religion - science. Of course that is much too complicated, even for the most sophisticated students, so we call the subject social studies for short. In chart form the scope of the field might be sketched in this way:

SOCIAL STUDIES

is

the study of

PEOPLE

carried on in order to help students understand

THEMSELVES and OTHERS

(accenting psychology, social psychology, and sociology)

in a

VARIETY OF SOCIETIES

(locally, in the U.S.A., and in other parts of the world)
in
DIFFERENT PLACES and at DIFFERENT TIMES
(geography)   (history)
as individuals and groups seek to meet their
NEEDS
(a variety of fields, including economics)
through many
INSTITUTIONS
(several disciplines, especially government)
as those human beings search for
A SATISFYING PERSONAL PHILOSOPHY AND
"THE GOOD SOCIETY"
(ethics, philosophy, religion, government)

I never showed students that chart until we had discussed our philosophies of teaching many times. It is not ideal, but such constructs or models have proved useful to me and I think to many students.

Because most of my students were well aware of the existence of a syllabus for each course in the social studies in New York City schools, we purchased such syllabi and studied them carefully, trying to discover their strengths and their weaknesses. In every methods course I asked each student to list the sections or units which they thought they could teach most easily and those which frightened them, an approach I had learned from Professor Spaulding at Harvard years before.

Then we went to work as a class on the topics which frightened the students most. For years it was the study of New York state and one of the cultural areas of the world — usually Africa. For several years the students then worked in small groups on units. When I finally decided that this took too much of the precious time at our disposal, I asked each student to prepare a series of five or six lessons on the topic which bothered him or her most.

Meanwhile we began to do a great deal of role playing in class. To introduce them to this difficult but highly productive form of learning and teaching, I usually taught several lessons on topics which they selected, with their playing the roles of different types of students.

Gradually I learned that role playing is more difficult for college students than for younger pupils because the older people at first are too self-conscious to let themselves go. And I soon learned that they were primarily interested in causing discipline situations to see how I would handle them, thus bringing to the surface a deep-seated fear of many prospective teachers. Often we stopped in the middle of a short lesson to discuss whether the lesson as it was being taught would ordinarily cause discipline troubles and why they were so concerned with this aspect of teaching.

Then I asked each of my students to teach for ten minutes or so in similar role playing situations. Usually I refrained from commenting on their teaching until their peers had aired their reactions, believing that it was easier for students to take criticism from their peers than from an older authority figure.

Sometimes the college students balked at the idea of teaching only a few minutes. They felt that they had merely gotten started when they were stopped. But in a short time we could learn about the student's voice, his ability to involve the pupils in a lesson, his poise, his knowledge of a topic, and his ability to handle questioning and discussion.

Not all the students reacted favorably to this method at first. Some of them thought it was silly. A few felt threatened by this approach. That was particularly true of those who had become adept over the years in reporting and/or discussion and had won their marks in school by such skills. But, after repeated experiences with role playing and discussion about it, almost all the participants recognized its relevance. Instead of merely reading about situations in the classroom, hearing about them, or even seeing them, these prospective teachers were experiencing them in simulated situations.

By playing the roles of different types of students, the participants usually gained some insight into the variety of human behavior and learning patterns which exist in every classroom. Often they began to understand the frustrations of slow students as they escaped, like turtles, into their shells or stuck out their quills, like porcupines. Or they learned how dull many classrooms are for the gifted.

Many prospective teachers also gained a better understanding of themselves through role playing and the subsequent analysis by the class, as well as through personal conferences, later, with the prof.

In order to make it easier, I usually asked the prospective teachers to select the topic and the situation which they would role-play for the first time. And to ensure a successful experience, we would often "replay" a situation.

I am aware that this method is not one which every college methods teacher should employ, but I found it an extremely useful device and used it a great deal. It was, however, not the only method we used. Sometimes we used a short film to stimulate discussion. Occasionally we used open-textbook lessons to show how important they are, especially with reluctant learners. Occasionally we stressed the use of the chalkboard or had panels.

One of my favorite approaches was the use of pictures mounted on cardboard and distributed to the class. One such lesson was based on pictures of the Russian people, cut from the pages of the *U.S.S.R.* magazine. As soon as the students had time to examine their pictures quickly and share them with their neighbors, the teacher would ask who had an interesting picture. Several hands would go up and student after student would show his or her picture, with the class talking about it. In the stack was a picture of a blonde in a Bikini on a beach. That raised the question as to whether it could be of a Russian.

At the end of the period all the pictures would be placed on the rim of the chalkboard and the class would attempt to summarize their conclusions about the variety of Russian people. This would be followed up by a reading assignment on the Russian people.

For several semesters I asked each prospective teacher to make a small collection of pictures on some subject to use in his or her student teaching — and later.

Social studies teachers are not likely to be very good artists and I certainly was not qualified to help them on that score. But I did work out several simple drawings which would help them in motivating thinking. One was the use of a simple drawing of a volcano. Students could then figure out how it erupted. Then the question could be raised as to how the American Revolution, World War I, or some other event was like a volcano.

Even a circle can be used frequently to illustrate an idea. For example, the increased wealth in the United States in the latter part of the 19th century and how that wealth should be divided, can be illustrated by this simple drawing:

U.S. Wealth in 1860   *U.S. Wealth in 1890*

How shall the new wealth be divided?

The circle is also an excellent device for talking about power.

From one of my college students I got the idea of drawing three faces on the chalkboard and asking students how they represented Metternich at three different times in his life. Eventually titles were given to each of the three faces, as in the drawing below:

**Metternich
in 1815**   **Metternich
in 1830**   **Metternich
in 1848**

155

WORLDVIEW

Then a discussion can ensue on the reasons for the different reactions by that famous European statesman.

One of the most helpful concepts for students to grasp is that all human groups divide on ways of meeting problems. In developing this idea a continuum is extremely useful. For example, the alternatives for Negroes prior to the Civil War can be elicited and put on a continuum like the one shown here:

What can we do as slaves in the 1840s and 1850s?

Suicide	Take Part in a Slave Rebellion	Attempt To Escape to Freedom	Try To Learn To Read and Write	Become a House Slave	Remain a Field Slave

In a similar way the continuum can be used on almost any problem facing a group of individuals or a nation.

As we worked individually, in small groups, and as a class, I tried to help these future teachers realize that their aims were central in their teaching and that they should not have more than two or three aims in a period. Beginning teachers are likely to attempt to do far too much in a short period of time, rather than concentrating on a few carefully selected and concise goals. I also emphasized that their aims should include attitudes and skills as well as knowledge, and I constantly checked lesson plans to see if they contained such aims.

As a result of a half century of research on the learning process, we know considerable about learning. We do not have "laws," but we have some generally accepted "rules." In every class we discussed those rules many times and I urged my students to save the pages in the methods book we used which listed such rules, even if they threw away the rest of that book. Here are 12 such rules:

People learn best

. . .when they are physically and emotionally comfortable, yet alert. This implies in social studies classes that:

156

. . .when they select or help select problems and goals of real interest to them. This implies in social studies classes that:

. . .through concrete, realistic, and predominantly firsthand experiences. This implies in social studies classes that:

. . .when they are challenged within the range of their abilities. This implies in social studies classes that:

. . .when they are stimulated emotionally as well as intellectually. This implies in social studies classes that:

. . .when they are involved in a variety of related activities. This implies in social studies classes that:

. . .when a new learning is related to an older learning. This implies in social studies classes that:

. . .when they have reflected on the meaning of their experiences and have participated in the evaluation of those experiences. This implies in social studies classes that:

. . .when learning is reinforced by meaningful repetition. This implies in social studies classes that:

. . .when they have a sense of personal and/or group achievement. This implies in social studies classes that:

. . .when there is an element of novelty and/or vividness. This implies in social studies classes that:

. . .when their knowledge leads to some action related to it. This implies in social studies classes that:

In my *Guide to Social Studies Teaching in Secondary Schools* and in my *Social Studies for the Seventies* several pages were devoted to these 12 statements, with room for the readers to write the implications for social studies teaching in the blank spaces.

Because of my belief in the centrality of teaching for

attitude reinforcement, improvement or change, I also developed a set of statements on attitudes. Some time during our work together we had bull sessions on our own attitudes, using my list to see how it applied to each of us. In order to stimulate this discussion, I always led off with one of my prejudices and tried to analyze how I had tried to overcome it. Then the students were more willing to expose their prejudices. Today we call this sensitivity training. I did not know that term but think I worked along those lines.

Lest anyone think that the students did not read much, I hasten to say that they did. We had some "common readings," such as Samuel Eliot Morison's *One Hour of American History,* John Kenneth Galbraith's Public Affairs pamphlet on *Economics,* and John Higham's *The Reconstruction of American History.* But much of the reading by students was individualized.

For a few years I used James Quillen's *Education for Social Competence* as a text, but it was long on theory and short on practice, so I developed many pages of practical suggestions for teaching and mimeographed them for my students and cooperating teachers. From those sheets came the volume *A Guide to Social Studies Teaching in Secondary Schools.* When I discovered that it was being used as the sole text in many colleges, I added more on theory in it in order to obtain a better balance.

Because so many of my students lacked background in a wide range of social studies topics, I wrote "background papers" on about 200 subjects and had them mimeographed. When the cooperating teachers began to ask for sets of those papers, I decided that I had something of value and selected 120 of them for a book on *Background Papers for Social Studies Teachers,* which the Wadsworth Publishing Company printed. That volume had perforated edges so the sheets could be torn out and inserted in folders.

Because I believed in the importance of keeping folders, I required each student to submit five such collections of materials, consisting of pictures, newspaper clippings, magazine articles and other data. In that way I hoped to start them on a life-long habit of collecting teaching resources.

DEVELOPING MODELS OR CONSTRUCTS

For the secondary school methods course and for the graduate workshop in elementary school social studies teaching, I developed a few models or constructs. Two examples are given here. The first is on ways of studying a family, anywhere in the world and at any time in history. It looked like this:

Different Aspects of a Family To Study

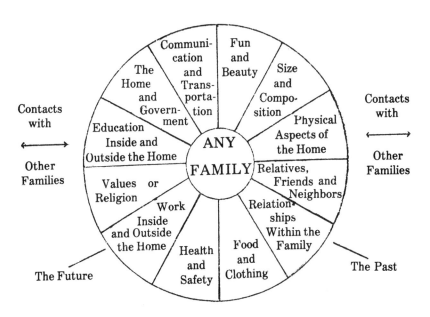

Another model or construct was developed on how to study a country or culture. It looked like this:

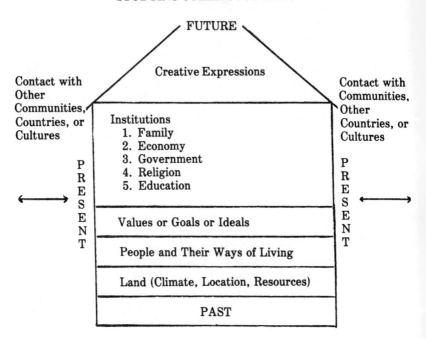

STUDYING OTHER COUNTRIES

FUTURE

Creative Expressions

Contact with Other Communities, Countries, or Cultures

Institutions
1. Family
2. Economy
3. Government
4. Religion
5. Education

Contact with Communities, Other Countries, or Cultures

PRESENT

Values or Goals or Ideals

People and Their Ways of Living

Land (Climate, Location, Resources)

PRESENT

PAST

SUPERVISING STUDENT TEACHING

Important as the methods course was, it did not compare with student teaching. As I have said before in this book, there is nothing like experience. But experience is not enough. One can practice a tennis or golf stroke and become a worse player. Practice does not always mean one becomes perfect. What one needs is experience under the guidance of competent teachers.

Therefore the selection of cooperating teachers was central to effective student teaching. In the beginning, I had no part in the selection of such teachers in the Brooklyn schools. Later I had some influence in the choice of such "models" for my students, largely through acquaintance with the heads of social studies departments or the assistant principals. After a few years some of my former students became cooperating teachers and I think the learning of the student teachers was vastly increased by working with two people whose approach was similar if not identical.

The developmental lesson, based on Herbartian principles, was in vogue in the Brooklyn schools throughout my years of work with student teachers. It was highly structured and not always conducive to learning. But it was entrenched and I had to struggle to use it — and then to show alternative ways of teaching. I required my students to use other approaches, and if their cooperating teachers balked, I told my students to say that I insisted that they teach a problem-solving lesson or a film lesson or a picture lesson. Then I would explain my position to the cooperating teacher when I arrived to observe my student in action.

Sometimes there were extraordinary results from this procedure. I recall one time, for example, when my student taught a lesson on Canada, using pictures pasted on cardboard. The lesson went well and the cooperating teacher was astonished. At the end of the class, he told me that he wouldn't have allowed the student to teach that lesson if he hadn't insisted that it was a requirement in the methods course. When I asked the cooperating teacher how he felt the lesson had gone, he replied, "It was GREAT." Then he asked, "But do you think the same lesson would work with those bastards coming in the door?" — a statement which some of them could overhear. I said I thought it would work even better with them and would be willing to try if he would lend me the class for the next period. That lesson with slower pupils excited them and the cooperating teacher became a convert to the use of pictures in social studies classes. By such approaches I tried to wangle my way with recalcitrant cooperating teachers. Usually I was successful; in a few cases I failed.

I tried to observe each student five times during the semester. They planned the first two lessons and I went over them, always 24 hours in advance, so that they could "internalize" any changes I made. On the other lessons they were on their own.

Much of the pre-planning of lessons and the discussions after my visits to the schools was done around the dining room table in my home. Often two students and I worked together. That was superior in some ways to the one-to-one counseling. The third party often gave his or her colleague security and often added ideas to the discussion. And the third party almost always learned something by listening to our discussion of a particular lesson.

Most of my students preferred the senior high schools over the junior high schools. But I worked hard to get as many of them as possible into the junior high schools. That was because I found more flexibility and openness to new ideas among the junior high school teachers, and because there were more job openings for my students at that level.

In order to encourage flexibility on the part of my student teachers and to get them away from the practice of using long sheets of paper for their lesson plans, which they placed on the desk and ignored or in which they buried their faces, I developed a plan for them to use 4 by 6 inch cards which they could hold in their hands. On each card was the material for one aim. Then, if the lesson changed direction, they could merely reshuffle the cards and not forget one of their aims. So far as I know, I am the only person who has insisted on such a procedure.

After every lesson and "post mortem," I typed up my comments. One copy went to the student teacher and another to the cooperating teacher, if there were no highly personal comments in it. The third I kept for my cumulative folder on that student. Years later my former students often referred to those summaries. Some even showed me the sheets they had kept. That seemed to me a superb evaluation of the method. Here is a typical report with all names omitted:

Helping Future Social Studies Teachers

Name of the Student Teacher   Name of the Cooperating Teacher
Name of the School and the Grade Level or Course

Lesson on World War I

As I said over coffee, I thought the lesson went well for a second lesson. Much better than the first one — and you have heard me say that every lesson isn't an improvement over the previous one. Congratulations. Keep going. Here are most of the points we discussed:

Best Points of the Lesson	Some Areas for Improvement
Good appearance.	Get to the filmstrip more quickly. They know it is there and want to see it. Your introduction was too long.
Gracious introduction of the visitor. Your invitation for me to take part made it easy for both of us.	
Excellent preparation. Knowledge of World War I superior.	Get THEM to read at the beginning. You did later.
Glad you tried a filmstrip lesson.	Remember to move around. You probably would have avoided that discipline problem if you had moved around.
Several questions from the class. Bravo. That's real feedback.	
Fairly wide participation.	Used Francesco too much. Give the others a chance.
Attempt to review at the end.	Perhaps undue attention to Russia's part.
Helping students with their reading without embarrassing them.	Tie summary into next assignment.
Board work as summary.	
Use of dates on chalkboard.	

Very glad you plan to do role-playing for the lesson on the Treaty of Versailles, with roles for Clemenceau, Wilson, Orlando and Lloyd-George. Figure out how to involve the rest of the class. It should go well. And my continued thanks to Mr. _____ (the cooperating teacher) for all his help.

Much as I enjoyed all my college classes, it was the personal conferences with the student teachers which pleased me most and made me feel I was accomplishing something worthwhile. One cannot remake a person in a semester or even a year, but there were many instances where the personal conferences did bring about important changes in the students. Sometimes the conferences turned into guidance clinics, marriage counseling sessions, or vocational guidance conferences. I recall scores of such situations. One was the request of a student to follow me around for two or three hours as I went to the store, the bank, and met with a colleague; he just wanted to see how I conducted myself outside the classroom. Another was an invitation to a student's home for a family party. We had discussed in class the many "hats" we wear and she wanted to see how I would perform in a totally different situation. I still chuckle over my attempt to converse with her grandmother, using my German to reply to her Yiddish.

Perhaps it would be interesting to some readers for me to conclude this account with my list of the eight chief characteristics of effective social studies teachers, merely mentioning them and letting the readers test them in relation to some outstanding teacher. They are: caring, communication ability, content, confidence, curiosity, creativity, commitment, and catalytic power.

CHAPTER 12

88 Nations and 50 States —
Travel Abroad and at Home

All of us carry tiny maps of the United States and of the world in our minds. Often they are distorted and large sections of them are blank. But gradually we begin to fill in parts of those maps through what we learn from films, television programs, reading, lectures, talks with people, and travel.

Each of those methods has been important in our family, but travel has played an especially important role in our education. I do not recall my first extended trip with my family, but it was undoubtedly when I was still very young, because we lived in the eastern part of the United States from the time I was four years old and made an annual trek to Indiana to visit relatives.

Our first car was a Lambert, but I do not remember it. I do, however, remember our model T Ford for which Dad made long, covered wooden boxes which were bolted onto the running boards. In them we carried our camping equipment. He also cut and hinged the front seat so that it would fold back and form a bed with the back seat. That was our crude but clever "mobile home" in the 1920s.

Traveling in an automobile was slow at that time,

especially going up the mountains in low gear. Often we boys tumbled out of the car and walked or ran alongside it, thus reducing the load and giving us a chance to stretch our legs and let off steam.

As we traveled, the person next to the driver held the Auto Guide and read directions to Dad, as road signs were still rare. "Proceed for three miles. Turn right at the Methodist Church. Follow a winding road for two miles and bear left at the fork in the highway." Such were the instructions in those road guides.

If we were not pressed for time, we would detour and visit a new state, for we "collected states" the way other children collected stamps, coins or dolls. By the time I was 12 or 13, I had been in at least 20 states.

Our contacts with people from abroad were frequent, too. My earliest recollection of a "foreigner" was the extended visit in our home of a Quaker minister from Canada. I was fascinated by his Indian moccasins and by the sassafras tea he prepared from roots found near our house. Father and Mother, however, were less intrigued with him, especially when his stay lasted for several weeks. Finally they suggested in a firm but friendly way that he move on.

In 1921 there was widespread famine in the U.S.S.R., with millions of people dying. Several relief organizations were formed, the best-known being the one headed by Herbert Hoover. English and American Quakers were active, too, and Dad was asked to direct the work of the American Friends Service Committee in a large area of the Soviet Union. Even though it meant leaving Mother and us boys, he felt that he should go in order to testify in a positive way to his religious beliefs, despite his firm opposition to communism.

His letters home were vivid. In them Dad described people dying in the streets and pictured corpses piled high, like cordwood, because there were not enough able-bodied men to bury the dead. He told how the American workers drew their shades in their dining room so that people could not see them eating. And he recounted how people sometimes kissed his boots in order to show their gratitude for the food he and his co-workers were distributing.

This was a gruesome introduction to the people of the world and my first lesson in human suffering, human understanding, and human generosity.

Japan was added to my world map in 1927 when my brother Carroll went there to work for *The Japan Advertiser,* an English language newspaper. His letters were frequent and fascinating, opening a window for me on Asia. But it was sometimes difficult for me to believe what he wrote, as I had acquired some of the American stereotypes about people in that part of the world. He wrote, for example, that almost every farmhouse in Japan had electricity. That was difficult to believe. I knew farmers in Indiana who still did not have electricity. How could *Japanese* farmers be more advanced?

THE TRIPS I TOOK ABROAD AND SOME COMMENTS ON THEM

My world travels started in the summer of 1937 with a "Grand Tour" of Europe, and I have been "tripping" around the world ever since then, visiting a total of 88 nations.

En route to Germany in 1940, I was able to visit Bermuda, Portugal, Spain, and Italy. Then, when I worked for UNESCO, I used most of my vacations to visit different countries in Europe.

In 1948 I was on the Survey Team on Education in Puerto Rico and at various times I have been in almost all of the nations in Latin America and in the Caribbean region.

In 1954 I went to Pakistan and en route home, saw several parts of South and Southeast Asia.

My most extensive and most interesting trip was the one in 1957 and 1958 to several new nations, a journey described in more detail in the next chapter.

More recently I have been back to Africa, and to Iceland, to Finland and the U.S.S.R., and to Kuwait, England, Switzerland, and Sweden.

All of these journeys have been for pleasure. But they

have also been an investment to make me a better teacher, a better writer, a better speaker, and hopefully a better human being.

With the exception of the summer in Pakistan, all my trips have been self-financed. For years I lived in a postage-stamp sized apartment with a low rent, depositing in a savings account the difference between what I paid and what I would have paid for a better apartment. That savings account I then used for travel. Usually I have had some writing assignment which helped to pay for trips and my talks on my journeys have brought some additional income. I suspect that some increases in salary came partly as a result of the background for teaching gained through travel.

I have always tried to do extensive reading about the place I intended to visit and I have taken voluminous notes on my reading, filing them topically in loose-leaf notebooks. When I reached my destination, I added other notes on these same topics. And upon my return home, I have done further reading, bringing "new eyes" to such reading as a result of my visits.

Often I have typed letters home, recorded on loose-leaf sheets so they could be inserted in a notebook by my family. For safety, I have kept carbons of these letters for myself.

Personal contacts are important when traveling abroad and I have almost always had help from the American Friends Service Committee and the Friends World Committee in acquiring the names of persons I could contact. Often I have been helped by other organizations, such as the Asia Society, the Japan Society, and the African-American Institute.

Upon arriving in a nation, I have always reported to the U.S. Embassy or the nearest U.S. consulate as a matter of record and of safety. Often some government official has become interested in what I wanted to do. On many occasions I have been helped, also, by the directors of the U.S. Information Service.

In many instances I have arranged for a short article to appear in the local newspaper or newspapers, telling about the purposes of my visit. Sometimes former acquaintances have seen such articles and contacted me. In other instances people I have asked for an interview have seen the article and have been "introduced" to me in that way.

When I have made an intensive study of a nation, I have bought books in several book shops and from the government printing office. Sometimes I have also asked the government to show me films on their country. That has saved me time, suggested places I should go, and given me a picture of their country as they are trying to present it.

First impressions are extremely important and so I have taken voluminous notes the first few days in a new locality before those initial impressions became commonplace. I have learned, also, to try to meet a wide variety of people in order to avoid a one-sided view of a nation.

Too many visitors abroad limit themselves to the large cities. To avoid that, I have frequently gone to the railroad station or bus station and purchased a ticket to some place two or three hours outside the capital or large city, visiting places tourists would never see.

It is amazing how friendly and helpful most people are when I explain what I am trying to do, especially if I have told them that I was collecting material for American teachers and school children. Almost always they have suggested other persons to see, even arranging for such interviews themselves. And on some trips my tape recorder has attracted people. I am certain that a Polaroid camera would do the same.

On almost all of my trips I have taken a large, illustrated map of the United States with me to use when talking with people about the U.S.A. And I have taken stamps and postcards to use or to give to children. In many cases they have reciprocated.

In most places I have made friends with the hotel porter or someone else on the hotel staff, having learned how helpful such persons can be.

Such are some of the ways in which I have learned to

gain the most in the limited time at my disposal. Often an outsider can see more than the local people see because the visitor is not hampered by the "blinders" of close association with a locality or culture.

But enough of such suggestions. Let us move on to brief accounts of some of the visits I have made to many parts of our planet.

MY GRAND TOUR OF EUROPE

My first trip abroad was in the summer of 1937. The U.S.A. was still in the throes of a depression, but I was anxious to see parts of Europe and I thought that would be a good "investment." So I planned a Grand Tour of Europe with a former colleague of mine, Ted Peters. We tried to see everything as we did not expect to return. Little did I know then that I would be "tripping" all my life and even living in England, France, and Germany in later years.

We landed in Plymouth, England, on July 4th, spent the afternoon at Stonehenge, worshiped that evening in the cathedral in Plymouth, and made our way by train to London that night. What a glorious 4th of July!

That summer we saw something of Scotland, England, Wales, Belgium, The Netherlands, Germany, and Switzerland. But the most memorable part of that trip was a week in a little Welsh town called Abercynon. Ted was active in the work camp movement and arranged for us to join a group there, living in the home of an unemployed coal miner and his family and working on their cooperative community garden project. The head of that work camp was Jack Hoyland, a prominent English Quaker who had lived several years in India and was a remarkable human being.

On Sunday morning we attended the Church of England, with its staid liturgical service and a handful of worshipers. Then, in the evening, we visited the Welsh Methodist Church, which was packed. And what wonderful singing, accompanied by the music of an old-fashioned pump organ.

The members of the work camp were from several countries and our visit was a rare treat for the villagers. They were so impressed that they asked us to autograph their hymnals with our names and the nations from which we came.

In Germany we were frightened by the influence of Hitler, especially in Nuremburg.

The father of one of my students in the Brunswick School was the editor of *The Greenwich Press* and he asked me to write a series of articles on our journey. That was my first venture in travel reporting.

VISITING PAKISTAN

While I was studying at Teachers College and living at International House, I was friendly with a young man from Pakistan. One evening in 1954 he called from Washington where he was working in the Pakistan Embassy. He reported that they were receiving hundreds of requests, especially from American teachers, for material on Pakistan, and that they did not have anything to send. He asked for my suggestions and I said I would call back the next day after I had thought about his request. At that time I suggested as a minimum program the production of a film or filmstrip, a short article about teaching about Pakistan, a packet of pictures, and a small book for students.

As a result of that conversation, the Pakistan government asked me to go to Pakistan to prepare some of those materials. I said I would be willing to go but unwilling to write officially for any government if they were to censor my material. They countered by offering to pay my expenses in Pakistan for six weeks if I would pay my way there and back. In return, they would not read any of my materials before they were published.

I agreed and spent six weeks in Pakistan that summer, visiting almost every part of that nation from Karachi in the south to Peshawar in the north, and then to Dacca and other parts of what was then East Pakistan.

I do not believe I have ever had "culture shock," but I

came close to it that summer as I saw the poverty, filth, and horrible housing in Karachi and Dacca.

Back home I began to write a short book on Pakistan. I completed much of it, but when I came to the chapter on government, I was stymied. Consequently I never completed that volume. Later events proved how unstable the government was, leading eventually to civil war and the formation of Bangladesh as a separate nation. I did complete the filmstrip and wrote an article for *Social Education* on "Studying Pakistan," which was reprinted for wider distribution.

While in Pakistan, I became acutely aware of the world-wide problem of refugees. At dinner one day with Gertrude Samuels, a feature writer for the *New York Times*, I asked her for an estimate of refugees in the world. She guessed it might be 10 to 12 million but she upped that figure to 15 million when she did a piece on that subject for the *Times*. Since that time there have been millions more, especially in Southeast Asia and Africa.

Visiting Some of the Nations of Africa

Mention the word Africa to most Americans and the pictures which will flash into their minds are likely to be deserts and jungles, gold and copper, wild animals and grass huts, and naked or scantily-dressed natives. That is not an exaggeration as I have tested it with students from the fourth grade through graduate school.

My knowledge of Africa was not quite as distorted as that when I made my first trip there in 1957, but it was sketchy and often incorrect. On a five-months tour at that time and again in 1961 I lived in the homes of Africans and visited them in schools, offices, factories, and hospitals. I talked with many of their leaders and scores of common people, gaining a reliable picture of Africa.

As a result of my experiences, I wrote *Profile of Nigeria* and *Profile of Kenya* for boys and girls and a booklet *Studying Africa in Elementary and Secondary Schools* for teachers. The most succinct statement of what I learned appeared in *Social Education* in 1960 in an article entitled

172

"The New Map of Africa in My Mind."

In that article I mentioned that my new map showed Africa as larger and more diverse geographically than it had been before. Even though I knew intellectually that Africa was four times the size of the United States, I had to travel by airplane, bus, train, canoe, paddle steamer, camel, and on foot to realize the enormity of that continent. I also had to retouch my map to include fewer deserts and jungles and more plateaus and savannas.

My new map also included a greater variety of people than the old one had contained. Now I could place on it the sophisticated city people as well as the nomadic tribesmen, plus representatives of such minority groups as the Lebanese, Syrians, and Indians.

My revised map also included more agricultural and industrial products than had appeared on the old map. It contained hillsides in Uganda covered with tea plants and plateau areas in Kenya planted with coffee bushes. It included the mammoth Kariba Dam in southeastern Africa and the giant plywood factory in Nigeria as well as the slag piles near the gold mines in South Africa and a score of new factories in Tanzania.

And there was more color and beauty on my new map than on the old one. There was the color of the kente cloth clothes of Western Africans, the beautiful wood carvings of the Kamba tribesmen in Kenya and the exquisite beadwork of the Zulus in South Africa, as well as the colorful hassocks made in Nigeria and sold all over the world as "Moroccan leather."

On my new map there were dancers on stilts in Liberia and the dancers of High Life music, but there were fewer drums than before. In my mind was the museum in West Africa where drums were being preserved as they were being pushed aside by electric guitars and juke boxes.

There were more clinics and hospitals, more schools and colleges, more community centers and libraries (including mobile libraries) on this revised map, too, and modern skyscrapers as well as grass huts.

Visiting Finland and the U.S.S.R.

For years I kept postponing a trip to the Soviet Union, largely because I did not speak Russian and realized that my French, German, and English would do me little good there. Finally I decided to go despite that handicap and the realization that I would be shepherded by a representative of Intourist, the government travel agency.

With this trip to the Soviet Union, I combined a brief visit to Finland. I found that country fascinating, with its thousands of lakes and its millions of pine, spruce, and birch trees. Helsinki struck me as conglomeration of old and new architecture, including the buildings designed by such famous modern architects as Alto and Saarinen.

Even more interesting was the planned suburb of Tapiola, the most beautiful and exciting of all the planned cities I have ever seen. It is nestled between outcroppings of rock and often hidden by evergreen trees. In the center of the community is a large, artificial lake and a shopping center. Nearby are attractive apartments and individual homes.

From Helsinki I traveled north to Jyraskyla and Korpalathi. The latter is a small but fairly typical village where many of the people earn their living by lumbering. I wanted to see it because we planned to include it in the fourth grade social textbook in my series.

After a short stop in Helsinki, I went by boat to Talinn in what was once Esthonia and now is a part of the U.S.S.R. In addition to seeing the old city and the rows and rows of new and rather poorly constructed apartment houses, I visited a Pioneer Camp outside the city.

From there I went to Leningrad, which seemed to me a combination of Paris, Venice, and Moscow, with its wide streets and beautiful vistas and its 600 bridges. This city was Peter's "window on the west" and long the cultural center of Russia. The ornate buildings of the Czars helped me to understand why Leningrad was also a center of revolution.

While there I spent considerable time in The

Hermitage, one of the great museums and art galleries of the world, with over 300 rooms, 30 of them devoted to Greece and Rome. But the highlight of my time in Leningrad was an evening at the ballet, seeing Tchaikovsky's *Swan Lake*, beautifully costumed and staged and beautifully performed.

Moscow was a surprise — an amazing city of 6½ million with scores of new office buildings and government structures, as well as hundreds of new apartment houses, some of them striking. In downtown Moscow there was considerable vehicular traffic, evidence that the Soviet Union was then entering the automobile age. But what changes that will demand, as there were only two filling stations in the entire city when I was there. Of course I visited St. Basil's, with its onion-top domes. And I was at Lenin's tomb when Nasser was there with Kosygin to lay a wreath.

Throughout my time in Moscow I kept insisting that I must attend some church services. Each time the guide postponed a decision. Finally I told her I was really curious about the Russian claims of religious freedom and wanted some proof. The next day she reported that she could take me to two churches! So we attended a Russian Orthodox service in the morning and the famous Baptist Church in the evening. The morning service was pathetic, with almost all the worshipers old women. But the evening service was a moving experience. There are approximately 50,000 Baptists in Moscow, but since they are allowed only one church, there are eight services on Sundays. The plain wooden structure was packed for the last service and there was a large choir, including some younger people. What impressed me most was the fact that these people were not there to be seen. Far from it in a country where formal religion is attacked — they were there to worship.

In Moscow I spent one day browsing in bookstores, getting my guide to translate passages and even pages from children's books for me. That was enlightening to me and a new experience for her.

From Moscow I went to Tbilisi, an industrial city, and

then on to Tashkent in Central Asia. There I wangled a visit to two collective farms and felt they represented agriculture in the United States in about 1900 or possibly 1920. I also persuaded my guide to take me to an early childhood center where I was impressed with the equipment, the doctor and nurse on duty, and the way in which the teachers treated the children.

When I left the Soviet Union, I decided that if I were to draw one picture which represented my impressions, it would be a dump truck with construction materials for the thousands of new apartment houses I had seen.

A Brief Visit to Kuwait

Kuwait intrigued me. There I saw nomadic tribesmen living in camel-hide tents as their ancestors had done for centuries and also people living in ultra-modern homes in Kuwait City, complete with air-conditioning and television. At the time of my visit Kuwait had the highest per capita income of any nation. It had a few multi-millionaires and many millionaires, plus many people with plenty of money in the local banks — or in Lebanon or Switzerland.

Kuwait is a country without taxes, although people have to pay a small fee for their water, to remind them that it is scarce and expensive, inasmuch as it is prepared at great cost in desalinization plants.

More than half of the people, however, are non-Kuwaitis, enticed there from places like Egypt, Lebanon, and what was formerly Palestine, to serve as doctors, lawyers, technicians, and teachers.

Most of the citizens of Kuwait understand the importance of education for the oncoming generation, and they have placed a high priority on money for schools, including a new and modern university. In addition, they send scores of young people abroad each year to study, providing them with stipends in addition to their expenses.

Nothing impressed me more, however, than the sight of hundreds of men in their long-flowing robes, sipping tea or drinking coca-cola in the evening out-of-doors as they watched the local television programs on sets provided by the merchants.

I was in Kuwait primarily to gather material for the fourth grade book in my textbook series, emphasizing the contrasts in life in that small land and the importance of petroleum. So I saw every stage in the production of oil from the petroleum rigs in the desert to the giant Japanese tankers which transported oil to different parts of the globe.

SOME OTHER EXPERIENCES IN TRAVELING ABROAD

Everyone who travels looks for special sights. But few people listen for the typical or unique sounds of the places they visit. On one of my trips I took a tape recorder and learned to listen for such sounds. In Morocco I leaned over the curb and recorded the click-clack of the donkeys' hoofs. In Liberia I recorded the shrill sounds of the crickets. In Ghana and in Nigeria I took down the high, sweet singing of the weaver birds. And in the Middle East I recorded the music in the bazaars and the calls to worship from the minarets, some by human voices and some by recordings.

Later, in Iceland, I learned that some countries are relatively quiet. Yet, even there, I found some special sounds like the whistles of the boats, the singing of the drunken sailors, the drumbeat of the rain against the buildings, and the thud of the ocean against the wharves.

Nobody has invented a smell recorder. How handy that would have been on my trips. In Iceland I could have recorded the smell of fish, the smell of the sea, the smell of grass and mosses after the rain, and the unbelievable stench of the whales as they were being carved up.

On my various trips I have also looked for the special colors of a given locality. Eventually I have tried to decide which colors predominated. For example, Paris seemed to say "Color me grayish blue." London called out, "Color me brown." Bangkok was a riot of color. "Color me green, orange, red, purple, and black," she seemed to say.

Everywhere I have gone I have found beauty, but beauty in different forms. In the colorful roofs of Bangkok I saw one type of beauty and in the deserts of Pakistan an utterly different kind. In the saris of India and the traditional costumes of the Japanese women I found beauty, too. Among the cities I have seen, Rio de Janeiro and Cape Town have the most beautiful settings.

There are scores of other recollections. The Lincoln Memorial at night is one of my favorite spots in the United States, while the Taj Mahal in India, and the Louvre in Paris, especially at night, with the Winged Victory of Samothrace ready to take off into space, are two favorites abroad.

As I have journeyed here and there I have often been struck by the fact that what is commonplace in one locality is rare in others. Visiting in Nicaragua in the home of a former UNESCO colleague, Joan Earle told me how she had asked her husband to go into the garden to pick some flowers for a dinner party. When he returned, he reported, "There's nothing there but orchids, Joan." Imagine having nothing for a dinner table decoration but orchids! In Nicaragua it would have been like using dandelions in the U.S.A.

Often I have heard Americans refer to the people of some parts of the world as lazy or explain their lack of production by the local climatic conditions. Of course climate has a tremendous influence upon people and their ability to work. But much of the trouble stems from the water-borne diseases which afflict a large part of the world's people. In my travels I began to realize that improving the world starts by improving the water in the wells of millions of villages.

On these trips I also began to realize the importance of the middle-level technicians in developing countries. This was impressed upon me in Pakistan where I rented a typewriter. Imagine my surprise to find the ribbon had been tied by some clerk who wanted to stop it from going round. And in Kuwait, of all places, the air-conditioners in the automobiles I used didn't work!

Politically I have always believed in the two-party or multi-party system. But after being in places like Kenya and Tanzania, I was no longer certain that two parties are always necessary or desirable, especially if there is opposition within the ruling party.

WHO ARE THE GREAT MEN AND WOMEN IN YOUR NATION?

As I traveled here and there, I found it provocative and revealing to ask people to name the 10, 12, or 15 most notable persons their nation had produced or about whom I should teach in the U.S.A.

The results of that inquiry were often fascinating. For example, in Denmark most of the people suggested for such a list were from the 19th century, whereas in Sweden they were mostly from the 20th, probably reflecting the period in which those two nations were at their height of influence. In Norway the majority of persons named were writers and I came to the conclusion that this was due to the long winter nights when the sagas of the Vikings were told and retold, thus encouraging future writers.

Altogether I have collected the names of national heroes in at least 25 countries. Here are the names for four nations:

England. Chaucer, Locke, Shakespeare, Milton, Dickens, Wordsworth, Shelley, Keats, Newton, Darwin, Harvey, Huxley, J.J. Thomsen, Adam Smith, and Elizabeth Fry.
Germany. Bach, Beethoven, Brahms, Wagner, Goethe, Schiller, Heine, Mann, Luther, Kant, Leibnitz, Ehrlich, Humboldt, Koch, Einstein.
The U.S.S.R. Dostoyevsky, Tolstoy, Turgenev, Gogol, Gorky, Chekhov, Pushkin, Moussorgsky, Tchaikovsky, Glinka, Rimsky-Korsakov, Pavlov, Pavlova.
India. Buddha, Maharia, Ramakrishna, Gandhi, Radhakrishnan, Kalidasa, Roy, Tagore, Jai Singh, Bose, Nehru, Naidu, Asoka, Khusrau, Ramanujan.

WHICH COUNTRY DO YOU LIKE BEST?

People have often asked me which country I liked best. Of course that is a question I can't answer; it is like asking a parent which child he or she prefers. Everywhere

I have gone I have met interesting and wonderful people — and difficult people.

But I do have favorite nations in special categories. For example, Switzerland and Guatemala are the most beautiful countries I have ever seen. One has a rugged kind of beauty; the other a manicured beauty. From an economic and social point of view, I rank Sweden and Denmark very high. They have their problems. Alcoholism and suicide are two of them. But one does not find the extremes of staggering wealth or wretched poverty in those two places that one finds in most nations, including the United States.

Seeing the U.S.A. in Better Perspective Through Travel

As a result of travel abroad I think I have been able to understand parts of our history as a nation better and to see the United States in better perspective.

For example, I realized for the first time in Guatemala the importance of good transportation in the U.S.A. Often in that tiny nation I saw families trudging along the roadside on their way to market. On the back of the father would be a contraption that looked like a small bookcase, with earthen vessels or pottery on each shelf. Beside him or behind him would be his wife, with a baby on her back and bundles in each hand. Scurrying along, trying to keep up with their parents, would be several children, each carrying something to market. What good would it do for such families, I asked myself, to produce more if they could not transport their products to market or find markets abroad for their increased goods? How badly they needed roads and trucks, as well as world markets.

In Liberia I saw the construction of the first major, hard-surfaced roads being built with aid from the United States. Then I realized how important our highways have been in tying our nation together.

As I have toured the world I have seen thousands of farmers scratching the soil with sticks or wooden plows, hoping somehow to eke out a livelihood from their tiny and often separated plots of land and from their starved soil. From these and similar experiences I have gained some appreciation for the fact that we in the United States have been fortunate in not having tiny plots of land to cultivate and that we had an Agricultural Revolution in the 19th century, with the development of Land Grant Colleges, agricultural experiment stations, and demonstration plots.

And when I visited a leper colony in Nigeria, supported in part by UNICEF, I was reminded that we had had several such colonies in the U.S.A. in former times but had been able to overcome leprosy and many other diseases because of our Sanitary Revolution and Health Revolution, events which are not stressed enough in our histories.

Is Travel Broadening?

Many people assume that travel is broadening and that world travelers are automatically world-minded persons. I have come to doubt that. If this is so, millions of soldiers who have been abroad and millions of tourists would be among our most international-minded citizens. And not all of them are.

In fact it is curious, and even distressing, to realize how defensive all of us become when we hear criticisms abroad of our nation. Sometimes we find ourselves defending policies abroad which we would decry at home, out of a misguided sense of patriotism. Perhaps it is a little like criticizing one's own family in the confines of one's home, but defending it when anyone outside says something negative about it.

What really counts in international travel is the internal security of the traveler and his or her ability to accept differences with equanimity and even at times with admiration. One of my favorite statements regarding the spirit in which one should travel was written by John Woolman in the 19th century about his visit to the American Indians. He said:

> Love was the first motion, and then a concern arose to spend

some time with the Indians, that I might feel and understand their life and the spirit they live in, if haply I might receive some instruction from them, or they might in any degree be helped by my following the leadings of truth among them.

What a magnificent statement. It could have been penned by an anthropologist.

Eleanor Roosevelt said almost the same thing, even more tersely, when she landed at New Delhi on her first trip to India. Asked by reporters to comment on her visit, she replied, "I have come to learn." Carlos Romulo of the Philippines said, "That unusual display of American humility did more to enhance American prestige in India than anything I can remember."

In my travels I have tried to keep those two statements in mind and to act accordingly.

CHAPTER 13

Visiting the New Nations and Interviewing Their Leaders

The most extensive and most exciting trip I ever took was in 1957-1958 to several of the new and emerging nations.

At the time I decided to make that trip, 20 nations had already won their independence. That meant that 650 million people (or one person in every five on our globe) had gained their freedom since World War II. This was a revolution unparalleled in history and it intrigued me so much that I decided to spend my sabbatical year on a tour of nations which had won their independence or would probably gain their political freedom in the foreseeable future.

Because of my long-term interest in biography and my conviction that the leaders of those countries would greatly influence the character of the new nations, I decided to concentrate on interviews with their top men. I was also aware of the practical consideration that those men were the George Washingtons of their countries and that the stories of their lives would never go out-of-date in any book I might write.

That trip lasted nine months, during which time I was able to meet about 25 leaders of independence movements, many of their associates and friends, and

183

some of their opponents.

In Africa I met Bourguiba of Tunisia, Mohammed V of Morocco, Nkrumah of Ghana, Kenyatta and Mboya of Kenya, Azikiwe and Balewa of Nigeria, Nyerere of Tanganyika (later Tanzania), and others. In the Middle East I saw Ben-Gurion of Israel, King Hussein of Jordan, and several leaders in Pakistan. In Asia I was able to interview Nehru of India, U Nu of Burma, Rahman of Malaya, family members and friends of Senanayake of Ceylon (later Sri Lanka), and Mrs. Magsaysay and close associates of the late Magsaysay in the Philippines.

Some Key Questions for the Leaders of New Nations

With me I took a list of 19 questions. I hoped that I would be able to use the same questions with each person so that I would have data for comparisons. However, the list proved far too long and eventually I used four key questions which were especially productive.

Jeannette Fuchs, a psychiatric social worker in the Brooklyn College Education Clinic, had suggested that I ask each leader what life was like when he was 14 or 15, a critical period in the life of any person. This was to prove a most revealing question.

Nehru was stumped by it for a moment and said so frankly. Then he remembered that he had been in England at that time in his life and began to talk about the influence of the English on his life and the fact that he had really lived in two worlds — Eastern and Western.

Ben-Gurion recalled that this was an "in-between" period in his life. The death of his mother when he was eleven had been a crushing blow. Not long after that, he moved to Warsaw to continue his studies. But he was more interested in politics than in education and he became active in the Poale Zion, a movement which combined Zionism with the goal of a socialist society. Soon after he began making speeches and taking part in demonstrations, he was picked up by the police and put into jail, from which his father eventually extricated him. Back home in Plonsk, he and his friends decided that they would emigrate to Palestine. One of them left soon and Ben-Gurion joined him there, later.

From my book, *Twelve Citizens of the World,* I got the idea of asking what persons had influenced these leaders most and what other influences there had been in their lives.

Most of the leaders referred to their fathers. This was a shift from persons in western nations where mothers are usually given the most credit by prominent persons. Probably the influence of fathers was most noticeable in the Middle East and Asia because boys there are turned over to their fathers early in life, after spending their early years almost exclusively with their mothers and other women in the family.

Diem of Viet Nam referred to his father as a prime influence, telling about his father's work in the royal palace as a tutor. Nehru mentioned his father first, adding the name of Gandhi in the next breath. Ben-Gurion also spoke of his father, although he mentioned his mother and her early death. Some of the other leaders, however, mentioned their mothers. This was true of Hussein of Jordan and Rahman of Malaya.

Asked about other influences, several of the men referred to their education abroad as an important factor in their lives. For example, Bourguiba of Tunisia referred to his years in France and his admiration for French culture. Nkrumah of Ghana mentioned the eight years he spent in the United States earning three degrees in that time. But he also referred to the racial discrimination he experienced there.

Several of the leaders spoke about the influence of independence movements and their leaders. Bourguiba spoke about Kemal Ataturk and the Turkish independence movement. Several mentioned Gandhi and the Indian struggle for freedom. Some also talked about the fight of the American colonies for independence in the 1770s. This was especially true of Nyerere of Tanganyika and Mboya of Kenya.

Books, too, were cited as an important influence. Mohammed V of Morocco spoke of the Koran, Bourguiba mentioned several of the works of French philosophers, and Ben-Gurion referred to the writings of Plato, Thucydides, and some of the Russian writers.

On most questions Ben-Gurion had a slightly different twist from the other men. Speaking of influences, he said, "The greatest influence on my life was life in Israel."

The third question which I posed was "What accomplishments are you most proud of since independence?" This evoked a variety of answers. Some were short and vague; others were lengthy. For most of the men, there were so many accomplishments that they were unable to cope with this broad question.

My fourth question was probably the most revealing. Almost always I phrased it in the same words: "I hope to return in 10 years. What changes do you hope I will find in your nation then?" That was a question suggested by my perceptive friend and colleague at Brooklyn College, Alfred Adler, and was intended to elicit their expectations. And it did!

Ben Gurion leaned his head against the back of his chair and his white hair blew in the breeze. Then he closed his eyes and began to speak. "Trees, trees, trees — millions of trees" was his first response. Then he referred to the construction of a port at Elath. Next he mentioned the water facilities of Israel. Quickly and with certainty he reeled off a list of changes which sounded like a five- or ten- year plan. But I noted that he skirted the question of relations with the neighboring nations.

When I asked Nkrumah that question, I added that perhaps I should come back in 15 years. "Oh, no, come back in five years and we will have plenty to show you," was his immediate and intense reply. I wondered if this did not reveal the influence of his years in the United States and his belief that much can be done in a short time.

Nehru's reply was utterly different as he launched into a philosophical discussion about the future and the nature of change. He was the only one who included references to foreign affairs, stressing the role that India would play as a neutral or uncommitted nation in the global struggle between the U.S.A. and the U.S.S.R.

WHAT CHARACTERISTICS DID THESE MEN HAVE IN COMMON?

When I set out on my journey, I assumed that these men would have much in common. I learned differently. Actually there was not much that they shared, each being a product of his country and his culture at a specific point in history.

All of them seemed to me to be leaders of lands of promise except King Idris of Libya and Hussein of Jordan. At that time the future of both of those nations seemed bleak. In my notes I referred to Libya as the U.N. Sandbox. Little did I know how quickly that nation would change in a few years as a result of the discovery of vast deposits of petroleum. Jordan's future seemed grim — and still does. It suffered from a lack of resources and the polyglot nature of its people. When I was there, it was composed of approximately 500,000 people from Transjordan, 500,000 from what had been Palestine, and 500,000 refugees. Can you imagine the difficulties of such a country?

Yet the men interviewed did have a few characteristics in common. When I asked people about their leaders and their characteristics, the first item mentioned was usually their integrity. Physical energy and "drive" were mentioned almost as often. Most of these leaders were also good speakers. The nature of leadership in an independence movement demands the ability to communicate, and work as head of a nation also calls for such a skill.

Several of their colleagues also spoke of these leaders as lonely men. And a few of their closest associates admitted that they were poor administrators. Probably the qualities needed for a leader of an independence movement are not those required of an administrator of a new nation.

A sense of the dramatic was another characteristic of several of these leaders. Ben-Gurion often capitalized upon the dramatic gesture, using this approach in his frequent trips to the Negev to dramatize the importance of settlements in that bleak part of Israel. Bourguiba was also a master of the dramatic, especially in his use of pantomime.

Timing was another skill of these leaders of new nations. Bourguiba was probably the outstanding example of this trait. How else can one explain his ability to win independence from the French without war? He had been the master strategist, able to negotiate compromises and to move at the most propitious moment.

Most of them also shared a background of imprisonment or exile.

Nearly all of these leaders were in a hurry, too. They knew that their job was to help their nation to pole-vault from the Middle Ages to Modern Times or from the bullock cart to the airplane. Diem of Viet Nam said, "Asian leaders are not permitted the luxury of plenty of time to study problems, debate about or carry on experiments to find the best solutions. This is especially true of Viet Nam, placed by geography and history in a most vulnerable position in the seething Asian volcanic mass." And how right he was, time would tell.

All of these men were wrestling with common problems, too — of transportation and communication, health and education, improved agriculture and industry, minority groups and the creation of a feeling of nationhood, urbanization and social erosion, and foreign relations. Some of them were beset with the enormous problems of languages in their nations, especially in India and in Nigeria.

Learning About the United States as A New Nation

One of the extra dividends of this trip which I had not expected was some insight into the history of the U.S.A. as a new nation. Here are some of the things I realized after visiting the new nations of the 20th century.

In 1789 the United States was a tiny nation, consisting of less than four million persons. And at that time we were surrounded by unfriendly or less than friendly powers, including England, France and Spain.

Our first government, under the Articles of Confederation, failed, and it was necessary to form a new and stronger national government. Even then one region did not join the United States. That was Vermont, which was independent from 1777 until 1794, with embassies in two nations abroad.

When it came time for us to select our first president, we turned to a general, much as some of the nations in the 20th century had done.

In the late 18th century we also had a language problem. English was a fairly common language but there was some pressure for making German the national tongue.

There was intense regional or state feeling, too, in the late 18th century in our land, with a stronger loyalty to the local unit than to the national government.

We also had our minority problem, with a significant group, the Tories, leaving or being driven out of the colonies and escaping to Canada.

Nor was internal rebellion unknown to us. We had our Whiskey Rebellion, which was somewhat analogous to the Cocoa Rebellion in Ghana in the 20th century. And we had our Alien and Sedition Laws which were something like the Deportation Acts in Ghana after its independence.

And not long after gaining independence, we were caught in a "Cold War" between the two powers of that day — England and France, which eventually drew us into the conflict of 1812.

I had learned in school about the many unifying factors which had made it possible for the United States to develop as a nation, but I had been unaware of many of the similar problems of the U.S.A. and the new nations emerging in the 20th century.

SOME REFLECTIONS ON MY WORLD TRIP

When I returned to the United States in the summer of 1958, I wrote a summary of my impressions from my nine months trip to the new and emerging nations. I mimeographed and mailed it to members of my family, colleagues in the social studies, and numerous friends. Monroe Cohen, the editor of *Childhood Education* received a copy and asked if he could reproduce it as an article in that journal. Here is that summary, edited slightly for this volume:

GLAD TO BE BACK IN THE U.S.A. — BUT UNHAPPY, TOO

After nearly nine months of travel in the new and emerging nations of Africa, the Middle East, and Asia, I am glad to be home. I return proud of my country, but more aware than ever that other people are proud of their nations, too, as they should be.

At the same time I am troubled about many aspects of my country. In the past two months I have seen the U.S.A. as others abroad see it and I am even more disturbed than before about many features of our national life.

As I return, I am proud of:

. . .the impact around the world of the idea of democracy as represented by such world-respected figures as Jefferson and Lincoln, Emerson and Whitman, as well as scores of other champions of democracy, and our interpretation of the idea of democracy as embracing all aspects of life — political, economic, educational, religious, and cultural.

. . .our virtual elimination of feudalism in agriculture when so much of the world is beset by problems of land tenure.

. . .our tremendous industrial output.

. . .our ability to provide a high standard of living for a large proportion of our people.

. . .our stress on the sacredness of lives, while so many people are still pulling rickshaws, being forced to carry "passes" because of their color, or toiling for a few pennies a day under abominable working conditions.

. . .our progress in providing health facilities, starting with a clean water supply, and our tremendous contributions to the world in medicine and health, including mental health.

. . .our development of social institutions, ranging from clinics and child welfare institutions to community councils and youth groups.

. . .our stress on the church as a social and humanitarian as well as a religious institution.

. . .our achievement in welding a nation out of the varied peoples who have come to our shores.

. . .our public library system, unparalleled in the world.

. . .our elimination of trade barriers within the vast expanse of the U.S.A.

. . .our remarkable systems of transportation and communication which have done so much to make us one nation.

. . .our long and, on the whole, creditable record in religious freedom.

. . .our progress in race relations in recent years.

. . .our growing maturity in cultural affairs.

. . .our concept of free public education for all children and youth.

. . .our development of scientific farming, with special emphasis upon agricultural colleges, demonstration farms, and county agents.

. . .our development of the idea of mass production, as it has helped to raise the standard of living of our people.

. . .our optimism and our belief that change is possible.

. . .our hard work, which has meant so much in raising the standards of living of most of our people.

. . .our extensive system of voluntary agencies.

. . .our high regard for women in most phases of American life.

At the same time I return grieved, troubled and disturbed about many features of our national life, such as:

. . .our hysteria over the recent achievements of the Russians in education and in science.

. . .our phobia about communism which blinds us to an objective appraisal of its appeal to many people and leads us to oversimplify international relations to a race between "their world" and "our world."

. . .our ignorance of most of the world and its people.

. . .our parochialism in assuming that the rest of the world should be like us and that we have little to learn from others.

. . .our inability to communicate in languages other than English.

. . .our export of so many tawdry films which millions of people around the world view.

. . .our support of decadent governments in so many countries.

. . .our naivete in believing that a parade of our wealth will make others want to be like us.

. . .our stress on freedom without linking it with justice.

. . .our reliance on military force and alliances to promote democracy and our neglect of IDEAS.

. . .our inarticulateness in expressing our democratic faith abroad — simply, tersely, dramatically, and boldly.

. . .our interminable debates over foreign aid and our concentration on military assistance.

. . .our inability to make more progress in race relations and in civil rights.

. . .our silly and futile attempts to compare our educational system with those of other countries.

. . .our timidity as educators in presenting the claims of our profession, championing the educational theories and practices which years of research have yielded.

. . .our concentration in recent years on math and science to the virtual exclusion of the social sciences and the humanities.

It has been exciting to be abroad these several months. I trust that experience has given me more perspective on my own country, too.

Some Results of My World Trip

Back in the United States I spoke many times about my trip. And after a short time in which to gain perspective on the journey, I plunged into the writing of a book on *Leaders of New Nations* which Doubleday published in 1959.

In that volume were accounts of 14 men. Only three African leaders were included at that time, however, and Doubleday asked me a few years later to revise the original edition, including the leaders of some of the African nations which had won their independence more recently. In that second edition we dropped the chapters on Diem and Senanakaye to save space. And we added chapters on Nyerere of Tanzania, Kenyatta of Kenya, Balewa of Nigeria, and Senghor of Senegal. For the new edition Erma Ferrari collaborated with me.

That journey added enormously to my background for teaching, writing and speaking, and challenged my thinking in many ways. For example, I became much more interested in economics and especially the economics of developing nations. I increased my interest in Africa. I think that my competence in devising curricula with an international dimension was also vastly improved. It also aroused my interest in other topics, such as the factors which contribute to a feeling of nationhood and some of the neglected aspects of U.S. history.

Those nine months were strenuous and demanding but they were also exciting and rewarding. Next to the year in Germany, that trip to the developing nations of the world was probably the most educational and significant period of my life.

CHAPTER 14

Encouraging American Educators To Teach About the World

Some people say that the world is growing smaller. In a sense that is so. In a world of superjets and instantaneous communication by satellites, the world seems to have shrunk, and it will grow smaller in the coming years. In fact the president of a leading airline company has asserted that we will soon be within two hours of any place on our planet by plane.

Yet in another sense the world is growing larger. Today we need to know about Burundi and Basutoland as well as Belgium and Brazil, and about Laos and Libya as well as Lebanon and Liberia. And we need to know a great deal about global interdependence and global problems.

Consequently the boys and girls in our schools today need to be prepared to live not only in their local communities and nations, but in the global community. In order to help in that task, teachers need to gain a cockpit view of the world rather than a porthole impression of it. Their knowledge of the world needs to be extended. Their awareness of global interdependence needs to be sharpened. Their sensitivity to the needs of their fellow passengers on spaceship earth needs to be increased. They need to develop a planetary perspective.

WORLDVIEW

Developing Global Frames of Reference

In order to help teachers, and eventually pupils, to grasp some of the salient features of our world today, I developed several frames of reference for living in the global community, sharing these widely with teachers and others in oral and written form.

One of those frames of reference concerned the people on our planet. In summary, it included the following points:

Most of the world's people live in Asia.

Most of them are nonwhite (in terms of color)

Most of them are farmers and fishermen and live in villages, although they are increasingly moving to cities.

Most of them are abysmally poor, and the gap between the rich and the poor is constantly widening.

Most of them are consequently ill-fed, ill-housed, ill-clothed, illiterate, and ill.

Most of them are non-Christians.

Most of them live under some form of socialism.

Most of them are working together, despite difficulties, in the U.N. and its related agencies.

That is a short statement about four billion people, but it has enormous implications. For example, I have often wondered what would happen if our legislators really understood those simple statements and their implications regarding trade, aid and education. Or what would happen to the curricula of our schools if teachers sensed the implications of those few phrases.

Usually I added a few other items to this primer on world affairs, pointing out, with illustrations, that

All of us have the same basic needs.

All of us are wrestling with the same, or similar problems.

All of us are rightfully proud of our nations.

All of us are interdependent and involved in the task of survival and of creating conditions of peace, justice and freedom for people everywhere.

Certainly no task is greater in our day than the creation of an international, global or world community. We face the alternatives of world suicide or world society, world

196

chaos or world community.

In order to help teachers, and through them students, I tried to sketch in thin pencil lines some aspects of the foreseeable future, recognizing the fact that no one can paint an accurate picture of the world of the future. Usually I mentioned these points, saying it would probably be:

A world of vastly accelerated transportation and communication.
A world of increased demands upon the limited sources of energy.
A world of increasing interdependence.
A world of gross inequalities and problems.
A world of more new nations, new world powers, and new political alignments.
A world of vast differences and some similarities among people.
A world of conflicts, with man's survival at stake.
A world of increased international planning and more powerful regional and international organizations.
A world of fun and beauty.

I also tried to suggest some of the characteristics of any community and then to apply them to the emerging global community of today and tomorrow. In abbreviated form, here are six such characteristics:

Any community needs "a common turf," and for the international community that is our planet. As the astronaut, Frank Borman, commented from space, "We are one hunk of ground, water, air, clouds, floating around in space. From out there it is really 'one world'."

Any community needs some common or shared ideals or values. Some of them exist in the sacred writings of all religions. Others have been stated in such documents as the Charter of the United Nations, the Universal Declaration of Human Rights, the Preamble to the Constitution of UNESCO, and the Declaration of the Rights of the Child — although the goals stated are by no means achieved yet.

Any community also needs some common symbols as outwards signs of belonging together. We have a few of them in the U.N. flag and buildings and in some international heroes, but we desperately need more of them.

Any community needs effective means of communication. Despite the multiplicity of languages and dialects which divide us, we are developing closer communication, thanks in large part to technological advances, such as television by satellites, cables, and the use in the U.N. of the top priority languages of French and English, and the five working languages.

Any community needs common institutions. In the world community today these include the 377 voluntary international organizations which have consultative status in the U.N., the increasing number of multinational corporations, and the U.N. and its agencies. More such international organizations will certainly have to be established in the future.

Last, but not least, any community needs community-minded individuals. In the case of the international community this means millions of people with a sense of loyalty to the human race.

Educating Internationally-minded Individuals

The schools of the United States and of other nations will never be able to do a great deal about the first five characteristics of a world community as stated above. But they can do much in the sixth category — the creation of internationally-minded individuals.

If one of the chief tasks of schools is to help develop persons with world horizons, then it becomes incumbent on some of us to spell out the type of persons we are trying to educate. One such statement was made by Brock Chisholm, the Canadian psychiatrist and first director-general of the World Health Organization, who wrote:

> In order that the human race may survive on this planet, it is necessary that there should be enough people in enough places in the world who do not have to fight each other, and who are the kinds of people who will take effective measures wherever it is necessary to prevent other people fighting.

In my doctoral dissertation on *World Horizons for*

198

Teachers, I wrote the following about the "Characteristics of World-minded Teachers." With little change, that statement could apply to others as well. Here is what I wrote:

The world-minded teacher is on his or her way to becoming:

. . .an integrated individual, skilled in the art and science of human relations and conscious of the wide variety of behavior patterns to which he or she may have to adjust.

. . .rooted in his or her own family, country, and culture, but able to identify with the peoples of other countries and cultures.

. . .informed about the contemporary world scene and its historic background and concerned about improving the conditions of people everywhere.

. . .convinced that international cooperation is desirable and possible and that he or she can help to promote such cooperation.

. . .an intelligent participant in efforts to improve his or her own community and nation, mindful of their relationships to the world community.

. . .clear in his or her own mind as to the goals of education for international understanding, conversant with methods and resources for such programs, and able to help create world-minded children and youth.

. . .buttressed by a dynamic faith or philosophy of life whose basic tenets can be universalized.

Since I struggled for months on that statement, the temptation is great to amplify it here. Except for a couple of comments, however, I shall desist. I do want to point out the importance in the first phrase of the word "becoming," lest people think that I am writing about a finished product rather than about people who are in the process of being educated. I want to stress, too, the fact that I was commenting not only about work in the world community but about the work one needs to do in his or her own community and country. And I want to reiterate the fact that all efforts are likely to fail unless a person has a philosophy of life, a faith, or a religion which helps him or her to persist despite disappointments. That view of life must be broad and inclusive rather than narrow and exclusive.

It is encouraging that some such internationally-minded individuals already exist. As Laurens van der Post, the South African liberal, has said:

> Already there seems to me to be in existence a new kind of human being who is living ahead of the meaning of our time, knowing only that meaning has to be lived before it is known, and that every step of the exacting journey has to be accomplished before new meaning can be discovered. Already in the world there are many individuals who are so strongly attacked by this contemporary reality that they experience inadequacies of their communities as sickness of their own physical being.

The economist and Quaker, Kenneth Boulding, has written along similar lines, saying:

> There is in the world today an "invisible college" of people in many different countries and in many different cultures, who have this vision of the nature of the transition through which we are passing and who are determined to devote their lives to contributing toward its successful fulfillment. Membership in this college is consistent with many different philosophical, religious, and political positions. It is a college without a president, without buildings, and without organization.

He then goes on to cite some of the graduates of this college. Among them he names Pierre Teilhard de Chardin, Aldous Huxley and H.G. Wells.

Some persons label such world-minded individuals as do-gooders, idealists, or visionaries. Far from it. Such internationally-minded individuals are the realists at this juncture of history.

Some Characteristics of the International Dimension of Schools

As I thought about education in general and the social studies in particular, it seemed to me that schools should help students at all stages of their development to live securely and creatively with themselves, with their families and friends, with people in their local community, and with people in their nation. But students need to be helped, also, to live with others in the international community. Some day they may need assistance in living, too, in space.

All these dimensions demand attention and I felt I should teach, speak and write on all of them. But I felt I had a unique background and a special mission for helping in the improvement of the international dimension of education.

In a 120-page booklet on *The International Dimension of Education,* written in 1970, I suggested 11 attributes of school programs emphasizing the world. Briefly stated, they included the following:

Any program should begin early and be based on self-respect. In almost all schools in the U.S.A. curricula are still built on the expanding horizons theory. Starting with the study of the families of the pupils, the program gradually expands to include a study of the local community, then the regions of the United States, and on to a study of the U.S.A. (This is usually limited to its history). By the sixth grade boys and girls are supposed to be ready to study Latin America or possibly ALL the countries of the world.

Perhaps this approach was satisfactory in its day, but by the 1960s it seemed to me archaic, obsolete, and even detrimental to children. Even primary grade children in that era had seen men on the moon, and the people of the world had entered their homes via television. Yet studies of the world and its people were postponed until the sixth grade!

To me it seemed important to have some study of the people in other parts of our planet carried on in the primary grades. Yet I was convinced that little learning, little understanding, and little appreciation of other people could be developed until children were relatively secure with themselves. They were not likely to respect others until they had begun to respect themselves, to understand others unless they had begun to understand themselves, and to appreciate others until they had begun to appreciate themselves. Therefore I postulated any

201

program about the world on the mental hygiene approach, helping boys and girls to live with themselves so that they could be free to live with others.

Any program about the world should foster the discovery by students of important concepts, generalizations, or "big ideas." Certainly the world is so vast that teachers can become lost unless some guidelines are clear. Therefore I began to work on some of the key ideas which I felt students should discover under the guidance of competent, concerned teachers.

These seemed to me to be some of those big ideas:

> We live on planet earth in the solar system. People are influenced by their environment and they adapt to it and change it.
> We have approximately four billion neighbors on planet earth. We have similar needs but meet them in many different ways.
> People everywhere live in families, although families differ.
> People everywhere live in communities.
> People live in nations.
> Groups of people who have common ways of living are called cultures. There are also many sub-cultures.
> People have unlimited wants and needs and limited resources. Most people depend upon others in meeting such needs.
> People everywhere have developed different explanations of "The Good Society" or the best way to live. We usually call such explanations a philosophy, a value system, or a religion.
> People grow up in a culture and learn the way of life of their group. Schools are one place where boys and girls learn their culture.
> People organize themselves into governments to do things they think they can do best in large groups. There are many different types of government.
> People everywhere are interdependent.
> People in all groups have problems and ways of working on them. Those ways vary from nation to nation.
> People everywhere are creative; they enjoy and create beauty and fun in similar and in different ways.
> Continuity and change are two important aspects of life anywhere in the world.

Any program should introduce students to selected segments of the world. For a long time I have supported the idea of selectivity in order to encourage depth-studies of a few topics rather than the superficial coverage of many themes. For example, instead of covering 150 countries in the 180 school days of a sixth-grade year, pupils should concentrate on 10 or 12 nations. Similarly pupils should study only a few selected families from different parts of the world, in the primary grades; and a few selected communities around the world, in the intermediate grades.

In general my approach has been to select these families, communities and nations from the eight cultural areas of the world: the Anglo-Saxon world, the Latin world, the Germanic-Scandinavian world, the Slavic world, Africa — south of the Sahara, the Muslim world, the Indic world, and the Sinitic (or Chinese) world.

Any program should stress people — their similarities and differences, and concern for others. In this regard I learned much from the late Lyman Bryson who once said that "The final test of international understanding is the ability to associate strangeness with friendliness rather than with hostility." It has long seemed important to me for elementary school children to concentrate on the study of people and primarily in their contemporary setting, whereas more attention can be given in secondary schools to institutions and to history.

Any program should accent changed behavior. Changed behavior seems to me to be the chief goal of education about the world. In large part such behavior consists of attitudes, skills and knowledge, but the greatest of these is attitudes.

Any program should emphasize feelings as well as facts. In recent years American educators have gone on a cognitive learning jag. Important as the intellectual side of learning is, no teacher should forget that learning involves the affective, or emotional, as well as the cognitive domain, including learning about the varied peoples of the world.

Any program should be continuous and cumulative and permeate almost every part of the curriculum. Obviously a large part of the work in the international dimension of education needs to be carried on in social studies classes, but every subject and every grade level should bear some responsibility for introducing students to the world. This is especially true of classes in literature, music and art. Co-curricular activities and the school library or media center also play an important part in such education.

Any program should utilize a wide variety of methods and materials. As we have already pointed out, different aims demand different methods. In addition, students learn in varied ways. Therefore any program about the world needs to be fostered by a variety of methods and materials.

Any program needs to be carried on by world-minded teachers. Little will be accomplished in this dimension of education if the teachers and administrators are provincial and prejudiced in their outlook. Therefore any effective program must include the pre-service and in-service education of teachers in order for them to gain a planetary perspective.

Any effective program must have the support of the school administration and the community. Persons concerned with promoting the international dimension of education need to bear in mind, also, that their efforts will fail unless they gain the support of the administrative officials and of important segments of the local community. Such support should include money to attend conferences and to purchase important teaching resources.

Any program should be experimental in nature and include evaluation. Major emphasis in schools upon teaching about the world is relatively new. Therefore such programs should be considered experimental, with as much evaluation built into them as possible. However, it should be clear that opportunities to test world-mindedness in action are rare. Therefore performance-based programs may be impossible to develop at present.

A WORLD-WIDE PROGRAM IN THE SOCIAL STUDIES

Most teachers do not have the background, time or

energy to develop extensive programs about the world. Therefore it seemed to me incumbent upon a few of us to suggest models which might be used in schools.

After years of thought and experimentation, I developed a plan which I called "The Twin-Spirals Approach" to the social studies, inasmuch as it emphasized education about one's own nation and about other parts of the world.

Eventually I realized that my plan could be used in any nation merely by inserting the name of that country in the left-hand column of the model or construct below, in place of the words U.S.A. I submitted this idea to the editors of *The New Era* magazine, which has an international readership and they published it under the title "A World-Wide Program in the Social Studies." That article included the following model:

Year in School	Basic Theme	Application Locally and to the Nation in Which the School Is Located	Application to Other Parts of the World
1. Individuals and Families Locally and in Other Parts of the Nation		x	
2. Individuals and Families in Selected Parts of the Rest of the World			x
3. The Local Community and Communities in Other Parts of the Nation		x	
4. Communities in Selected Parts of the Rest of the World			x
5. The Nation in Which the School is Located: Emphasizing the Contemporary Scene		x	
6. Selected Nations in Other Parts of the World: Emphasizing the Contemporary Scene			x

7. History and Problems of the Nation in Which the School is Located	x	
8.	x	

9. A Two-Year Study of the Eight Major Cultural Regions of the World		x
10.		x

11. The Nation in Which the School is Located — In its International Setting	x	
12. Contemporary Problems of the Nation and of Other Nations	x	

So far as I can ascertain, this is the first such suggestion of a possible world-wide program in the social studies which has ever been made.

SOME TEACHING ABOUT THE WORLD IN VARIOUS COLLEGES

In addition to my work at Brooklyn College, I was fortunate to be able to do some teaching about the world in other institutions.

One of the American representatives at the first UNESCO Seminar in 1947 was Rees Hughes, the President of the State Teachers College in Pittsburg, Kansas. In 1953 he invited me to serve as a special consultant to their Workshop on International Understanding, a pioneer effort at that time. Then I spent a summer at the University of Illinois teaching social studies methods, with a special emphasis upon the world. That invitation came through the efforts of my friend of C.P.S. days, Herbert Zim. In both those institutions I worked primarily with elementary school teachers.

Then, in 1956 and 1957, I served as director of workshops on Education for International Understanding at Penn State. That invitation came through the efforts of another friend from C.P.S. days, Elton Atwater. From my standpoint those were nearly ideal workshops. Each of them lasted six weeks, with six credits for the participants — three in education and three in political science. We had spacious quarters and a wonderful coordinator, Rose Cologne, who was helpful in many ways. Our workshops also included a few full-time students from abroad and several visitors from overseas.

Our first week in the summer of 1957 was devoted to various aspects of The World Community Today, the second to Latin America, the third to Africa, the fourth to the U.N., the fifth to the Middle East, and the sixth to the "back home projects" on which each participant worked. At the end of the fourth week, when the momentum of most workshops lags, we went to the U.N. headquarters in New York City for three days, plus two days of the weekend for sightseeing and fun. In addition, I was responsible for a university-wide public lecture by an invited speaker each week and for a weekly film festival. Each of the lectures drew several hundred persons and on one occasion we had 800 school superintendents from all over Pennsylvania in our audience.

When Dr. Tewksbury died during the fall semester of 1958, Margaret Cormack, of Brooklyn College, and I taught his large class in International Education at Teachers College, Columbia University. Included in that group of approximately 120 students were people from 30 nations. For two semesters I also taught that course on Saturday mornings. Reaching such a large and representative sample of teachers from all over the world was thrilling and challenging.

WORKING WITH ORGANIZATIONS INTERESTED IN WORLD AFFAIRS

One of the most effective ways to promote an idea is to work through existing organizations, capitalizing upon their wide contacts. Over the years I have worked with at least 15 organizations interested in world affairs.

One of my most gratifying experiences was as an educational adviser to the School Affiliation Service of the American Friends Service Committee. That program was developed after World War II to aid schools in Europe. At first it consisted largely of gifts sent to schools by American students. Eventually, however, it grew into a broad-based program of exchanges between "matched schools" in France and Germany and the U.S.A. Correspondence between teachers and between students was encouraged and exchanges of scrapbooks, picture books, tapes of assembly programs, and studies of local communities were fostered. Traveling representatives in Europe and in the United States and conferences of teachers and students on both sides of the Atlantic were held to improve programs. Eventually the program was extended to other parts of the world, but it remained primarily a Europe-centered undertaking.

To me this idea of affiliations is one of the most promising practices in international education because it involves students, teachers and parents, and encourages long-term friendships and exchanges. I have long wished that every boy and girl in American schools could take part in several such affiliation experiences, somewhat along these lines:

College years: Africa and/or Asia

High School years: Africa and/or Asia

Junior high school years: School in a country in which the language American students are studying, is used. Mexico or France?

Intermediate school years: School in an English-speaking nation: England or Australia?

Primary grades: Rural and city school exchanges or inner-city and suburban school affiliations

It seemed to me tragic when the American Friends Service Committee abandoned this program owing to lack of funds. It is something which needs to be taken up again by some organization.

At various times I have served on the international relations committees of the Association for Childhood Education, the Association for Supervision and Curriculum Development, the National Council for the Social Studies, and the National Education Association. In two of those groups I was also the chairman.

One of the best ideas we developed as an Association for Supervision and Curriculum Development Committee was to prepare several one- or two-page mimeographed leaflets of practical ideas for teachers, such as "Sources of Pen Pal Correspondence," and "A Self-Survey by a School of the International Dimensions of Its Curriculum." We prepared 16 such leaflets. We also submitted them to the editors of state educational journals, several of whom used them in their publications, giving us access to a broad audience.

For two terms I also represented the Association for Supervision and Curriculum Development on the United States National Commission for UNESCO.

Probably the most satisfying experience in such organizational work was as chairman of the International-Intercultural Committee of the Association for Childhood Education International. For three years that alert group of educators accented ethnicity in the U.S.A. and the international dimensions of school programs in a project called NEIGHBORS UNLIMITED. Several publications were prepared and an article written for the *Branch Exchange* each month for that entire period, highlighting some aspect of the project. To culminate our program, our committee viewed 75 films and selected 25 to recommend to schools in a brochure printed by the A.C.E.I.

In the 1970s I became chairman of the Liaison Committee for the UNESCO Associated Schools Project in the U.S.A., a program which had been dormant for several years in our country until it was revived, largely because of the enthusiasm and expertise of Adelaide Kernochan. For several months we concentrated upon a cluster of schools in Connecticut, but in 1975 we expanded the program to include schools and colleges in eight states.

In 1975-1976 I served as the educational consultant to the Scholastic Magazines in the preparation of ten remarkable color, sound filmstrips on the world, with the photographs by Ken Heyman, on such topics as Water, Tools and Machines, and Shoes and Hats.

SOME JOBS WHICH NEED TO BE UNDERTAKEN

There are many tasks which need to be undertaken in international education. Here are a few:

1. Develop a broad program of affiliations with schools overseas.
2. Develop a national clearing house for curriculum materials and the sale of materials on world affairs.
3. Launch a research program to develop evaluation devices in the international dimension of education.
4. Prepare scripts for educational television on various phases of education for international cooperation.
5. Film a series of brief classroom teaching situations featuring different phases of education for international understanding, for use primarily in teacher education programs.
6. Prepare a booklet on introducing children to the world in primary grades.
7. Develop "teams" of consultants on world affairs teaching for various regions of the U.S.A.

AN INTERNATIONAL EDUCATION GROUP

As I look back over the years of work on the international dimension of education, I realize that one of the most stimulating groups I ever worked with was a small, informal group of persons in the New York metropolitan area which Carleton Washburne brought together in the late 1940s. We limited the group to 17 or

18 persons interested in international education. Once a month we had dinner together on a Friday evening followed by a discussion. Occasionally we had a guest who would introduce a topic with a 15- to 20-minute presentation, but often a member of the group would lead our discussion.

The membership varied from year to year but included such persons as Alice Miel, Harold Rugg, David Scanlon, and Donald Tewksbury of Teachers College; C.O. Arndt of New York University; Sam Everett and Park Beck of the City College of New York; Juul Altena of Newark State College; Dorothy Gray and Max Eckstein of Queens College; and the Washburnes, Alfred Adler, Margaret Cormack, Ursula Kirkpatrick Springer, Eunice Mathew and I from Brooklyn College.

Each year we organized a conference on international education for the teachers in the metropolitan area, with 700 to 800 in attendance.

After Washburne's retirement, Dr. Arndt and I served as chairmen of this group until it merged with the local chapter of the World Education Fellowship.

CONCLUSION

Over a period of many years I have tried to serve as a catalyst for change in urging schools and organizations to examine their programs to determine how they can most effectively promote a better understanding of the people on our planet. There have been disappointments and set-backs, but there have been many stimulating assignments, many wonderful opportunities to work with people in various groups, and some progress on many fronts.

There have also been some gratifying statements about my part in nudging educators in new directions. In his volume on *New Frontiers in the Social Studies,* John S. Gibson wrote that "Kenworthy has blazed many frontiers in the social studies, especially in the area of education in world affairs. More than anyone else he has pioneered in this dimension of education."

In his volume on *Strategies for Social Science Education,* Bruce Joyce referred to me as "a one-man curriculum center for international education." And Oliver Caldwell wrote that "when the story of teaching about Asia in American schools is written, the name of Leonard Kenworthy will be recorded as one of the earliest and one of the most effective pioneers."

CHAPTER 15

Writing, Speaking, and Consulting with Schools

People have frequently asked me when I started to "write." I am not sure, but it may have been when I was in the fourth or fifth grade and Grandma Holloway and I exchanged letters, parts of which were in poetry or doggerel. About the same time I had a collection of 300 or so discarded spools of different shapes and sizes which I pretended were people. Sometimes they were Congressmen; often they were members of the local Friends Meeting. At other times they were shopkeepers, with old cigar boxes as their "stores." For *Our Town* I produced a small newspaper, complete with articles, headlines, and editorials.

On my fifth-grade report card there was just one notation. It said, "Shows much ability in written expression."

While I was at Westtown, I was the winner in a Peace Essay Contest, with several books as the prize, including a beautiful set of Shakespeare's writings, which I still value. Then there was my work as editor of *The Brown and White.* In my senior year I wrote an essay for Master Carroll's English class describing Easter Sunday at the Irving Street Meeting in Washington, with President Hoover in attendance. Master Carroll thought the essay worth publishing and it appeared in *The Westonian,* the

213

alumni journal, under the title "With Hoover at Quaker Meeting." That was my first printed piece.

At Earlham I continued to write, serving as managing editor of *The Earlham Post* and editor of *The Sargasso.* My most rewarding writing, however, was the essay for the Zelah Van Loan Essay Contest for North America, in which I won first prize and a check for $300. In our journalism class we were asked to try to get one article published, and I was fortunate in getting my piece on "Henry Clay in Richmond, Indiana in 1842" printed in the *Indiana Magazine of History.*

The summer after my graduation from Earlham I stayed at home with Dad and Mother and during that time I wrote a series of articles for *The Penn Weekly*, a Sunday School magazine for Quaker young people. All of those articles were biographies of Quakers: Lord Lister, the founder of antiseptic surgery; Benjamin West, the painter; William Bradford, the printer; John Bartram, the naturalist; and John Greenleaf Whittier, the poet and antislavery leader.

My first book, *The Tall Sycamore of the Wabash,* has already been mentioned. It was written when I was 22.

For people interested in writing, there may be some clues in what I have just reported. If there is any advice for young and aspiring writers, it is to write about something with which you are familiar and hopefully in a field in which there is interest but not too many writers. Another suggestion is to get your early efforts published in school or specialized publications rather than trying to write for *Harpers* or *The Atlantic Monthly.*

By the middle of the 1930s, two or three articles and several book reviews of mine were being printed each year, mostly in educational and religious periodicals. The book review is a particularly good approach for beginners as there are more opportunities for them than for articles. And the reviewer gets the books free, as well as the recognition for the printed work.

From that time on my writings fell into four categories: Quakerism, biography, education, and the social studies, with considerable overlapping of the last three categories.

SOME WRITINGS ON QUAKERISM

Over a period of approximately 40 years, I have written many articles, several pamphlets, and two books on Quaker subjects. Together they constitute a respectable little library on Quakerism.

The two books were *Toward a Fourth Century of Quakerism*, a series of essays, and *Quaker Leaders Speak*, a compilation of quotations from the works of Robert Barclay, Pierre Ceresole, George Fox, Elizabeth Fry, Carl Heath, Rufus Jones, Thomas Kelly, Isaac Penington, William Penn, John Wilhelm Rowntree, John Greenleaf Whittier, and John Woolman.

Three of the pamphlets were reprints of articles which had appeared in *The Friend* and other Quaker periodicals: "George Fox — Seeker," "Going to Meeting," and "The Society of Friends in 1970." Other pamphlets are: "John Bright — Nineteenth Century Humanitarian," "World Citizens for a World Community," "Meditations Around the World," "Introducing Children to the Life of the Spirit" (the Western Yearly Meeting Annual Lecture), and "The Peace Testimony of Friends." In addition to the titles in the Speaks Series which were bound together in the book *Quaker Leaders Speak*, I added leaflets about Kenneth Boulding, Howard Brinton, Douglas Steere, and Elton Trueblood in 1975.

Some of these writings were also translated into other languages for use by Quaker groups. For example "Going to Meeting" was printed in Japanese and in French, and most of the Quaker titles in the Speaks Series were printed in Luguli for use by Quakers in Kenya.

The list of articles I have written is too long to include here, except for those which were reprinted as leaflets, as indicated above.

SOME BIOGRAPHICAL WRITINGS

My interest in biography probably began when I was

eight years old. Since that time I have devoured thousands of books. Of special interest to me have been the writings of Catherine Drinker Bowen and Irving Stone.

One of my first published volumes was entitled *Twelve Citizens of the World*. Printed in 1953 by Doubleday, it had a good sale for many years. In it I dealt with Ralph Bunche — Champion of Colonial People, Pierre Ceresole — Dreamer with a Shovel, Mahatma Gandhi — Non-Violent Revolutionary, Toyohiko Kagawa — Practicing Christian, Fridtjof Nansen — Modern Viking, John Boyd Orr — World Hunger Fighter, Eleanor Roosevelt — Defender of Human Rights, Domingo Faustino Sarmiento — Citizen of the New World, Albert Schweitzer — Doctor in the Jungle, Sun Yat-sen — Creator of Modern China, Arturo Toscanini — Maestro of World Music, and Mathilda Wrede — Friend of Prisoners. That book was also translated into Indonesian.

As I read biographies and autobiographies and the works of famous people over a period of many years, I usually marked striking passages. Then I tried to distill their wisdom into eight-page pamphlets, with one page devoted to a brief biography of the person and seven pages to his or her writings, topically arranged. This came to be known as the Speaks Series and includes the 16 Quaker leaders already mentioned, plus 38 others. They include such persons as John Dewey, Kahlil Gibran, Thomas Jefferson, William James, Alan Paton, Albert Schweitzer, Rabindrinath Tagore, Laurens van der Post, and Walt Whitman. On a few of those leaflets I had the assistance of friends.

There have been many expressions of appreciation for those leaflets, but the two I prize most highly were from Albert Schweitzer and Alexandria Tolstoy. Schweitzer scrawled a note in English, saying, "You have done an extraordinary job in selecting quotations from my writings." Alexandria Tolstoy wrote, "May I express my deep appreciation for the wonderful work you are doing, including the leaflet on my father."

SOME WRITINGS ON TRAVEL AND WORLD AFFAIRS

As I have traveled in various parts of the world, I have done some reporting. Articles have appeared in several magazines and newspapers, with the majority appearing in *The Progressive* and *The Christian Science Monitor*. Several books and pamphlets have also grown out of these journeys.

On my jaunt through South America in 1953, I was impressed with Brazil and I hurried home to try to capture on paper some of impressions of that continent-like country in a book for boys and girls. My "book" was only 28 pages, but it appeared in the Lands and Peoples Series of Holiday House and in *Books In Print*, so I assume it fits into that category.

From my two trips to Africa I gained enough background to write introductory volumes called *Profile of Kenya* and *Profile of Nigeria*, plus three pamphlets and several articles.

In the early 1960s officials in UNESCO asked me to draw upon my years of work with that organization and my background in teacher education to write a book which they called *Telling the U.N. Story: New Approaches To Teaching about the United Nations and Its Related Agencies*, a volume which was published in several languages.

Late in the 60s I drew upon my interest in different parts of the world in curriculum to begin a series of booklets for the Teachers College Press called the World Study Guides. By 1975 that series included nine titles: *Free and Inexpensive Materials on World Affairs, Studying the World, Studying Africa, Studying China, Studying India, Studying Japan, Studying the Middle East, Studying South America,* and *Studying the U.S.S.R.* The sales have not been overwhelming, but they seem to have served a useful purpose.

Perhaps the story of the first of them will prove interesting to some readers. In a course in curriculum at T.C. with Dr. Stratemeyer, I wrote a term paper on "Free and Inexpensive Materials on World Affairs." There was so much valuable material in it that I thought it a shame to relegate it to my files. So I had it mimeographed and sold it privately. The response to it was encouraging and there were several other editions of it over the years until the Teachers College Press felt there was enough interest for them to print it. On two editions I had the help of others: my nephew, Tom Kenworthy, and a former student, Richard Birdie.

The volume on world affairs, however, which was the most fun to prepare was a picture book with 470 black and white illustrations, entitled *Three Billion Neighbors*, published by Ginn and Company for boys and girls. For it I pored over thousands of photographs from many sources.

Of all my writings on world affairs, a short article in *The Progressive* attracted the most attention. It was called "A Primer on World Affairs," and stressed the fact that most people live in Asia, live in villages, are farmers and fishermen, and earn less than $100 per person per year. It was reprinted in over 100 publications and excerpts from it were used by Adlai Stevenson in one of his campaign speeches. And for that article I received $15!

Some Writings on Education and Especially the Social Studies

Because of my primary interest in education and in the social studies, most of my publications have been in those fields, including a few already mentioned in this chapter. Articles have appeared in several journals, but most of them have been in *Childhood Education*, *Educational Leadership*, the *Proceedings* of the Middle States Council for the Social Studies, *Social Education*, and the *Social Studies*.

Some of my articles have been reprinted in other journals and in books of readings; the one that has been used most often is an article from *Social Education* on "Studying Other Countries."

My first book on education appeared in 1958 from the

presses of Harper and Brothers and was called *Introducing Children to the World: In Elementary and Junior High Schools.* That volume was a pioneering effort in the field of international education and was frequently cited in other works, even though its sales were never large. It is still the only book of its kind ever published.

Most of my early work in education was with secondary school people, but it was not until 1962 that I wrote a book for teachers at that level. That volume was called *A Guide to Social Studies Teaching in Secondary Schools.* Originally it was intended as a supplementary volume to existing books in methods, stressing practical classroom applications of theories. Much of the material was presented in outline form and the readers were often encouraged to fill in blank spaces in the book. When I discovered that it was being used in several colleges as the only text in methods courses, I added considerable material on theory. That book is now in its third edition and being used in many college classes and in social studies workshops.

Then, in 1966, the Wadsworth Publishing Company printed another volume of mine called *Background Papers for Social Studies Teachers.* It contained 120 two-page summaries of outstanding issues in social studies teaching and was printed so that teachers could tear out each page and insert it in their files. That was another innovation in educational publishing.

Officials of the Wadsworth Company wanted a methods book for elementary school teachers in the social studies but waived their rights to such a book when they learned that I was to become the senior author of a textbook series published by Ginn and Company, which included plans for a methods book. In 1969 such a book appeared from the presses of the Blaisdell Company (the college division of Ginn) with the title *Social Studies for the Seventies: In Elementary and Middle Schools.* That volume has been used widely and a new edition appeared in 1973. Today it is a publication of the John Wiley Company.

In the early 1950s I served as Vice President and then President of the Middle States Council for the Social

Studies and was responsible for two issues of their *Proceedings.* One was on *Social Science Frontiers* and the other on *Asia in the Social Studies Curriculum.* Both were pioneering efforts at the time.

Of the many pamphlets I have written, the one which has attracted the most favorable comments is a booklet on *The International Dimension of Education.* It was prepared for the World Conference of Education, held in Asilomar, California, in 1970, and was printed by the Association for Supervision and Curriculum Development. It is probably the most comprehensive and yet the most concise statement I have ever written in that broad field. It also appeared in an Arabic edition and at the present writing it is being considered for translation into Portuguese and Spanish.

Then there have been many "units" for teachers, many of them mimeographed and sold at cost to teachers. In fact there have been so many such publications that a friend of mine tells a story about them. In their family they sometimes concoct what they call St. Peterisms, or comments which people are supposed to have made to St. Peter when they accosted him at the gates of heaven. One would ask, "Is there a golf course here?" Another would inquire, "Where is the Methodist section?" And Kenworthy is reputed to have asked, "Has anyone done a unit yet on heaven?"

In the mid-seventies I began a series of small books for children profusely illustrated, which I call my "fun books." The first of these was *Camels and Their Cousins,* published by the Harvey House. The second was on *Soybeans: The Magic Beans,* written in collaboration with Laurence Jaeger, and published by the Julian Messner Company. The third was on *Hats Around the World,* also published by the Messner Company.

Some Comments on Writing

I have never pretended to be a great writer but many colleagues, friends, and students have consulted me about writing. In many cases I have read their manuscripts and made comments about them, or reacted to their plans for publications. Perhaps some of the comments I have made to such persons will prove helpful to some of the readers of this autobiography.

As I have already said, write about something in which you are a specialist.

Remember, too, that writing is hard work. Few people know how much time and energy it takes. It means giving up many television shows, movies, or holes of golf. So don't expect to toss off an article over the weekend or a book during your summer vacation.

After you have decided on a topic, gather all the material that you can; become saturated in your subject. Half of the battle is over if you have done lots of research. And if you know in advance the topic on which you are going to write, you can save material for months. You may be amazed by the number of references that come to your attention if you have your topic in mind.

I have found it useful to break down a big job into small, manageable sections and to set myself realistic, short-term goals. Then I encourage myself by checking off each small part of the total plan as it is completed.

Look for practical applications or examples of your ideas. Then pepper your manuscript with them. Harry Rivlin once wrote that "The two most important words in education are 'for example'." And how right he was.

Surround yourself, too, with the best "tools" you can find. That will save you many hours of work. Such tools include a Thesaurus, an electric typewriter, and such references as a geographical dictionary and a biographical dictionary (or their equivalents in your field).

Finally, try to write simply and briefly. Most beginning writers and far too many educators try to sound profound and brilliant. It is far better to try to write as you speak. Then people are more likely to understand what you say. Some people even find it helpful to use a tape recorder in the early stages of writing in order to maintain a conversational approach.

If you do write, I hope it brings you as much fun and

satisfaction as it has given me over a period of many years.

SPEAKING HITHER AND YON

I have not kept an accurate account of the number of speeches I have made, but in 40 years of speaking, it must have been at least 1500. I have been ready to board a train, bus, or airplane for almost any place in the United States if the group in that locality was working on a curriculum problem in the social studies or in the international dimension of education.

Sometimes the groups I have visited have been small, such as local curriculum committees or social studies departments. But often they have been large, especially in the fall when I have spoken to city-wide or county-wide audiences. The largest group I ever addressed was a regional meeting of teachers in a "tabernacle" in western Ohio, with 5000 present. I was scheduled to follow the Cleveland Symphony Orchestra and was loathe to be placed in that spot. So I suggested to the chairman that he declare a ten-minute break after the concert to enable people to stretch. Knowing how overwhelming that experience might be, I wrote out the first few sentences of my talk. That preparation was wise as I learned when I faced a sea of faces and was almost breathless for a moment. With my written material in front of me, however, I was able to proceed until I had gained enough composure to speak freely from my notes.

There have been other frightening occasions. One occurred in a town in Illinois where I was temporarily ensconced in a dressing room while a quartet from Chicago "warmed up" the audience upstairs. I reached into my suitcase and pulled out what I thought were my speech notes. But it was the wrong talk! Frantically I searched for the right notes — and found them. But from that time on I kept the original copy of any speech in my coat pocket and a carbon in my suitcase.

Some talks, however, have turned out to be thrilling occasions. For example, I recall the experience of substituting for Abraham Ribicoff, who was then head of the U.S. Office of Education and a well-known speaker. In the men's room before my talk, I overheard a man asking, "Who is this bloke from Brooklyn?" Apparently the audience felt sorry for me or were surprised that I did as well as I did, for I received a standing ovation that evening from 1600 principals of elementary schools from all over New York state.

The topics on which I have spoken to large, city-wide or county-wide audiences have varied, but the most frequent talk has been "Education for the 20th and 21st Centuries." Since I learned early in my career that I was a dud at telling jokes, I decided not to do this and fall on my face. Instead, I have used something resembling shock technique. Often I have told audiences about the many schools I have visited which were doing a superb job of preparing boys and girls to live in 1900 — or 1925 — or 1950, but not for the latter part of the 20th century and the start of the 21st century. Then I have tried to suggest the kind of world in which students might be living in the year 2000, asking listeners if they were really preparing students for such a world.

In order to involve the listeners and to be practical, I have almost always posed questions, such as "What are you teaching about the land under the oceans — the 75 % of the earth which is still largely unexplored?" Or, "What contacts with people from other nations are you providing for your students?"

In such groups I have tried to include suggestions for nearly all grade levels and subject fields at some point in my talk. Special references to the important role of librarians have sometimes drawn applause, as they are almost always ignored by speakers.

The titles of talks to local, regional, and state-wide social studies audiences reveal much about the current interests of such groups over the years. Among such topics have been "Richer by Asia," "The New Map of Africa in My Mind," "Trends in the Social Studies," "Problem Solving in the Social Studies," and "Beyond Values Clarification." One talk I have given many times over a period of several years is "The Many Methods of the Social Studies."

Wherever possible I have asked for time for questions and discussion in order to involve the participants and to give me valuable "feed-back."

Wherever I have traveled, I have tried to find time to see something outstanding locally, whether it was the unusual art gallery in Toledo, Ohio, the giant redwoods in California, the Norris Dam in Tennessee, or the Truman Library in Independence, Missouri.

CONSULTING WITH SCHOOLS AND SCHOOL SYSTEMS

There have been many opportunities to serve as a consultant to a single school or to a school system. Often those jobs have involved all-day meetings with a curriculum committee or with teachers of the social studies. Occasionally they have included three or four meetings with a group, spaced over a period of several weeks, with the local group working on a project between visits.

During the burst of interest in "the new social studies" in the 1960s, there were a few assignments which were even more ambitious, involving the creation of new programs in school systems. One of them was in Great Neck, New York, where I worked as a consultant for several months on the revision of their social studies program from the kindergarten through grade six. That job included a six weeks workshop one summer with a small group of key teachers, as well as several meetings with all the elementary school teachers in that city system.

An even more ambitious undertaking was in Fair Lawn, New Jersey, where I worked two summers with small groups of teachers on the revision of their social studies curriculum, K-12.

On similar assignments I worked with the school systems of Locust Valley, New York; Greenwich, Connecticut; Vicksburg, Mississippi; and Manhasset, New York.

In 1968 I was ready to summarize what I had learned from such work. The article I wrote was on "Changing the Social Studies Curriculum: Some Guidelines and a Proposal." It appeared in *Social Education* and was widely reprinted.

As I have worked in various places, I have received some special citations. There was no special significance to them, but they were fun. One came at the conclusion of the UNESCO Seminar in Paris, when I was made an honorary citizen of that city. A similar honor came in Quincy, Massachusetts, made famous by the Adams family, at the conclusion of a workshop there. And at the end of a week's workshop for the Association for Childhood Education in Kentucky, I was made a Kentucky Colonel by the governor.

One more experience in the total curriculum process remained for me to explore. That was the preparation of a series of social studies textbooks. In the next chapter I will deal with that ambitious project.

WORLDVIEW

CHAPTER 16

Textbooks as Scapegoats or as Many-Splendored Publications

It was Thanksgiving time in the early 1960s and I was attending the annual convention of the National Council for the Social Studies. In some spare time I was wandering up and down the aisles of the exhibits. As I turned a corner, someone called out "Professor Kenworthy." I didn't know the man, but since he was stationed at the booth of Ginn and Company, I assumed he was a salesman. "I'm glad to see you," he said, "for I read your recent article in the *Phi Delta Kappan* on "Ferment in the Social Studies" and thought it was GREAT. In fact, I gave copies of it to all our staff."

Obviously he was not a salesman; he was an executive. Then he introduced himself as Ben de Luca, the head of the elementary social studies division of Ginn. After a brief exchange, he asked me whether I had ever considered the preparation of a textbook series. I replied that I had not only done so, I was in the process of discussing such a possibility with a publisher. A little taken back, he hastily said, "Oh, don't sign up with any company until we have had a chance to talk with you."

Apparently he meant what he had said, for within a week he and Henry Halverson, one of the top executives in Ginn and Company, invited me to meet with them in New York City. And within a few weeks I had signed a contract with Ginn to become the senior author of a series

227

of textbooks to be called The Kenworthy Social Studies Series.

When I told a few close friends about this venture, some of them complimented me; others commiserated with me. Little did I realize then how long it would take to produce such a series. Nor did I know the headaches and heartaches I would have in the years ahead, as well as the joys that lay in store for me.

Textbooks as Scapegoats or as Many-Splendored Publications

Of course I was conversant with many textbooks. I had read them, reviewed them, and used them. I knew some of their strengths and also some of their limitations. I also realized that every evil in teaching is blamed on textbooks. They have been and still are the scapegoats of education.

Obviously it is difficult to write a good textbook. It is even more difficult to produce a series of them, particularly in the social studies. The road on which a textbook writer rides is filled with potholes and pitfalls. The author must know his subject and be able to stress its salient aspects. He must be accurate and include the latest interpretations of his topic or era. He must write simply and dramatically and yet produce a volume which every student supposedly can read — and in most classes there is at least a range of three grades in reading ability. He must please people in the north and south, the east and west. And he must meet most of the demands of Blacks, Chicanos, Indians, Italians, and other minorities. In addition, he must steer a course between the Superpatriots and the World Federalists. Above all, he must remember the teachers on textbook adoption committees, for they are the ones who select textbooks. So the volumes must be lavishly illustrated, be filled with activities to keep students (and their parents) busy every evening of the school year and not cost more than the books of competing companies.

Pity the poor textbook writer; his lot is not an easy one.

Today's textbooks are far from perfect, but they are vastly superior to those produced 50, 25, or even 10 years ago. Compared with textbooks produced in other nations, ours are far better in content, in interest to children, in learning theory, in illustrations, and in binding.

In fact, most of the criticisms leveled against textbooks should be leveled against the teachers who use them. Critics say that textbooks are slavishly followed, but that is the fault of those who use them, rather than the authors. Critics likewise maintain that textbooks are used as the sole learning tool. Yet all textbooks and teachers' manuals urge instructors to use a wide variety of methods and materials.

When judiciously used, I see nothing wrong with good textbooks. In fact, I see much merit in the use of a text or several texts as the "common reading" of a class, supplemented by other materials. As I see it, a textbook is merely a launching pad or a diving board for learning. It is a means to an end, not the end. Well-conceived, well-written, well-edited, well-illustrated, and well-printed, a textbook can be a many splendored publication.

A few teachers do not need a textbook, although they certainly need some "common readings" for their classes. But such teachers are rare. An overwhelming majority of elementary school teachers do not have the time, the background, the energy, or the imagination to devise their own courses of study and to find all the supporting resources that are needed.

Because of these and other considerations, the senior authorship of a social studies textbook series, K-8, appealed to me as a way of helping hundreds of teachers and thousands of pupils to become acquainted with the people of the United States and with persons in other parts of our planet. To me this was an opportunity to pioneer in new curricular patterns and to nudge social studies education in new directions.

I knew there would be difficulties in producing such a series for I had talked with the senior authors of three textbook series in the social studies which were already on the market, and with two experts who had resigned in disgust before their series were completed. So I started my work with trepidation and yet with high hopes.

Planning a New Social Studies Textbook Series

As I saw it, a series of social studies texts for the 1970s and 1980s needed to take into account such factors as the knowledge explosion of our times, new insights into the learning process, research in the social and behavioral sciences, the increasing interdependence of people and nations, the new knowledge about the possibilities of introducing boys and girls at a very early age to basic social science concepts, and the increased emphasis upon problem-solving, discovery learning, or inquiry.

In a 27-page document I outlined the overall design of such an innovative series. That plan was then submitted to the social science consultants of the series, the Ginn editors, and the prospective authors. It was modified only slightly by them. It highlighted the following approaches:

A Twin-Spiral Curriculum, Emphasizing the U.S.A. and Other Parts of the World. In place of the archaic concentric circles approach to the social studies, I envisioned a twin-spiral approach which would concentrate almost equally on the U.S.A. and on other parts of the world. Pupils would first study families in the United States and then families in other parts of the globe. In the third grade they would study American communities and in the fourth grade, communities in several other parts of our planet. In the fifth year they would study the U.S.A. as a nation, with the following year devoted to a study of a few other carefully selected nations. In the seventh and eighth grades, students would study the U.S.A. in more depth, devoting a year to decisions in the U.S.A. today and a year to decisions in the U.S.A. in the past.

A People Centered Program. Ideas, institutions, interrelationships, and ideals would be stressed, but they would be incorporated in the study of individuals and groups. People would be the center of our program.

Gradually boys and girls would begin to see the U.S.A. and the rest of the world as a giant workshop, laboratory, and playground for the people on our planet.

Accenting Minorities. As a correlary of the foregoing point, I wanted to emphasize the importance of minorities, especially in the U.S.A., thereby making many students proud of their heritage and developing in others respect for the contribution of all ethnic groups to American life. I planned, also, to accent minorities in other parts of the world, revealing prejudice as a world-wide problem.

Based on Selectivity for Depth. From the beginning, I recognized that it would be impossible for pupils to study scores of families, communities, and nations without encouraging superficiality. Therefore I determined to be highly selective in the examples to which students would be exposed. That meant the development of criteria for selection.

Emphasizing the Present, But Including the Past. Studies of learning indicate that young children have a great deal of difficulty with the concept of time, as they largely live in the here and now. Therefore I decided to accent the present, especially in the primary grades, introducing just enough history to explain the present. But at the fifth and eighth grade levels we would stress the past.

Avoiding Undue Repetition in U.S. History. In almost every school in the U.S.A., students at the fifth, eighth, and 11th grade levels spend an entire year on U.S. history, approaching it the same way each time. I resolved to avoid such repetition in my series. In the fifth grade we would spend only a half-year on history and concentrate on five decades — the formation of our nation, the Jacksonian era, the Lincoln era, the Theodore Roosevelt era, and the Franklin D. Roosevelt era. Then, at the eighth-grade level, students would wrestle with 22 of the great decisions in our history, such as Who Shall

Control North America? United States or Divided States? and Shall We Drop the Bomb?

Stressing Urbanization. Because of the growing urbanization of the United States and of many other parts of our globe, I wanted to emphasize cities in the third, fourth, and seventh grades, with the stress in the junior high school year on contemporary problems in cities.

Highlighting Attitudes, Skills, and Values. Highly relevant knowledge would be stressed in each textbook, but I was determined to concentrate upon the formation of attitudes, the acquisition of skills, and the examination of values. In the words of Phil Wass, our seventh grade author, we would help boys and girls "to make sense out of life — your life and the lives of other people around you."

Promoting the Discovery of Concepts and Generalizations. Early in our planning a group of us made a rigorous study of the major concepts in the various social sciences and constructed a chart for the series, showing at what level an idea would be introduced, where it would be extended, and where it hopefully would be "fixed."

Drawing Upon All the Social Sciences. It also seemed important to me to capitalize upon the tremendous gains over the past 50 years in all the social sciences, mining the rich ore of anthropology, social psychology, and economics, as well as geography, history, and political science. And because I had learned from anthropology and from gestalt psychology the need for total situations or "wholes," rather than segregated segments, I wanted to use an interdisciplinary rather than a multidisciplinary approach as much as possible.

Utilizing Many Methods, with Emphasis upon Inquiry. The increased emphasis upon problem solving, inquiry, or discovery learning in recent years in the social sciences was completely in accord with my philosophy of social studies teaching and so I planned to use a variety of methods in the texts and in the Response Books, but to emphasize inquiry as the most important method.

OUR PLAN BEGINS TO TAKE SHAPE

The officials of Ginn and Company responsible for this project agreed to our overall curriculum design. Some were even enthusiastic about it. In addition they agreed to print some of the books in sections as paperbacks; to provide a readability test on each volume before it was published; to field-test the various manuscripts; to furnish a stunning graphics program for the series; and to develop multi-media packages for each grade level. They also endorsed the idea of Response Books, incorporating much inquiry learning, to take the place of the old-fashioned workbooks or "busybooks" for pupils.

The project as planned was ambitious, relevant, innovative, comprehensive, and exciting. The skeleton outline, with the titles of books as they finally appeared, consisted of the following, with the title for the series changed to the Ginn Social Science Series:

The Ginn Social Science Series

Grade or Level	The United States	Other Parts of the World	Supplementary Volumes	Other Materials
K	You and Me (Study Prints)			Response Book and Teachers Guide
1	Families Are Important			Response Book and Teachers Guide
2		Families Are Everywhere		Response Book and Teachers Guide
3	We Live in Communities			Response Book and Teachers Guide
4		Everyone Lives in Communities		Response Book and Teachers Guide

5	One Nation		Response Book and Teachers Guide
6		Eleven Nations	Volumes on France, Italy, and Turkey	Response Books and Teachers Guide
7	We Are Making Decisions		Response Book and Teachers Guide
8	Decisions in United States History	Two volumes on Reliving the American Experience	Response Books and Teachers Guide

SELECTING THE PERSONNEL FOR THE SERIES

Of course the choice of authors for the various books was crucial.

Because of her knowledge of the broad field of the social studies, her special competence regarding the primary grades, and her ability to deal brilliantly with concepts and inquiry learning, Ben de Luca and I both wanted Charlotte Crabtree of the University of California at Los Angeles to be the senior author of the primary grade books. Fortunately she accepted our invitation and was helpful with many aspects of the program in the ensuing years.

It was my contention that textbooks could be improved if well-known writers for children could be enticed into joining our team. They would certainly be able to write in simple, dramatic, non-textbook style. And any deficiencies they might have in the social studies field could be overcome by other members of the team. I was therefore glad to persuade Sonia and Tim Gidal to join us. They had already produced more than 25 volumes in the *My Village* series of the Pantheon Press and were willing to spend many months in various parts of the world, gathering material and taking pictures of families and communities for the second and fourth grade volumes.

Fortunately we found other persons with outstanding abilities as authors of other books. Peggy Shackelton brought a deep understanding of children, a sensitivity to people and situations, and a charming style to the first-grade volume and to a part of the second-grade book. Charles Quigley was then coming into prominence in the social studies field and he agreed to prepare the manuscript on communities in the U.S.A. for the third grade.

Ben de Luca asked me to wrestle with the fifth-grade book on the U.S.A., in which we would combine for the first time an emphasis upon the contemporary scene with some history of our nation.

For the sixth-grade book we were lucky to obtain the services of Bani Shorter and Nancy Starr to write on *Eleven Nations.* Bani had lived for several years in India and Turkey and written extensively and beautifully for boys and girls. She also knew other parts of the Middle East and Asia. Nancy had just returned from several months in the U.S.S.R. and was also conversant with several parts of Europe. I wrote the chapter on Nigeria and helped a great deal on some other parts of the book.

For the seventh grade we enlisted the help of Philmore Wass of the University of Connecticut. Phil was well-known for his work in economics and for his concern about contemporary problems and problem-solving. For the eighth-grade volume we were able to obtain George Shaftel, who combined the talents of an historian with those of a free-lance writer. George had also gained a national reputation for his work in role playing, in collaboration with his wife, Fannie Shaftel.

For several years Robert Edgar of Queens College of the City University of New York had been working with junior high school students, especially in inner-city schools, using autobiographical accounts of Americans of different backgrounds to whet the interest of students in U.S. history. I called upon him to utilize this rich background to produce two volumes of source materials, called *Reliving the American Experience.*

We were also fortunate in the authors for the Response

Books and the Teachers Guide.

Some Problems in Producing a Textbook Series

No enterprise of this size and scope can be produced without problems. We had them — plenty of them. Some were small. Some were tremendous. Some were horrendous.

Not all the authors I have mentioned were in the starting lineup. Some of them joined the team months or even years after our work had begun. Unfortunately we had to terminate our agreements with a few writers for various reasons. Of those whom I invited to be on the team, only two were not up to their assignments. Both of them were well-known writers, but they were older women who did not seem to be able to adjust to changes in the United States and to the problem-solving approach. Several other persons, however, caused us trouble. One even sued the company when her contract was terminated.

Some of the authors had marital troubles. Some had financial difficulties. All of them had disagreements with their editors. Sometimes I felt like a marriage counselor, a financial adviser, and a negotiator, as well as a social studies specialist and writer.

In the main we had four types of difficulties which I will mention here to demonstrate that publishing is a perilous profession and to alert readers who may contemplate such writing to some of the frustrations they are likely to encounter.

First was the tremendous turnover in the administrative staff of Ginn and Company. In the years I worked on the series, six different persons headed the elementary social studies division and/or our project.

Second was the continuing problem of the role of the senior author. Was he responsible for all the work on the series and a partner in the decision-making processes or merely a consultant, "name," or "front"? From conversations with other senior authors, I surmise that this is a perennial problem.

236

Third was the question of the division of power in Ginn and Company between the social studies and the graphics department. It seems to me that their decision to make the art department sovereign in all matters related to the illustrative program on the series was an horrendous mistake and one which damaged the series.

Fourth was the on-going problem of all publishers — the lack of enough expert editors. After years of experience with many editors in several publishing companies, I have decided that a good editor is like a piano accompanist. Such a person should be able to subordinate himself or herself to the soloist and support the singer rather than competing with or drowning out the performer. There are a few editors who work in that way. Such persons work wonders. But many editors are really technicians rather than editors. Working with them is a nightmare. Two illustrations should be sufficient to show what I mean.

After an editor had worked on one chapter of a book for months, she was finally asked to show us what she had done with it. Instead of improving it, she had turned a basically promising account of a city in Switzerland into a tourist brochure, picturing the town as a cute, postcard village with snow falling like sugar on its quaint rooftops, rather than as a big, bustling, beautiful metropolis.

In another instance, I had slaved for nearly two years on a book which two consultants had praised highly. But when I received the editor's comments, there were 19 pages of single-spaced, negative criticisms, and one sentence of praise — "I liked your opening statement." At that point I contracted pneumonia.

Many changes can be worked out amicably between authors and editors if they sit down and work together on a manuscript. I recall with pleasure one such example when Wally Becvers and I sat for ten hours and reshaped a chapter on which the editor had struggled for weeks with great damage to the original manuscript in my opinion.

But there comes a time when production schedules make further changes impossible. Consequently authors

237

sometimes have to accept editorial changes which do not please them or meet their high standards.

Celebrating the Production of the Series — and Helping Sell It

In 1972 the series was finally published. To celebrate the occasion, I gave a party in New York City which 60 friends and members of my family attended.

Then I went "on the road" to tell people about the series. Despite some shortcomings, I felt it was the best series of social studies textbooks, K through 8, which had ever been published. So I was glad to discuss it with groups of teachers in several parts of the U.S.A.

Everywhere I went the Ginn salesmen treated me royally; I thoroughly enjoyed my contacts with that unusual group of human beings.

Meanwhile 25 other publishers had been at work on series of new social studies texts. The competition, therefore, was unbelievable, especially at a time when school boards were cutting back on appropriations for new books and interest in "the new social studies" had begun to falter.

Despite the frustrations and disappointments, I was still glad that I had undertaken this tremendous task and had been able to bring it to fruition.

CHAPTER 17

Some Reflections on Quaker Schools

For over 300 years Quakers have been specialists in schools. At various times and in various places they have established and administered educational institutions ranging from nursery schools to colleges and adult education centers. Some Friends have pioneered in such fields as coeducation, the teaching of science, the inclusion of "practical subjects," the education of Indians and Blacks, work projects, and the study of international affairs (including experiences abroad for students).

Even though some Quakers question the need for such schools and colleges today, new ones continue to be founded. Of the 65 elementary and secondary schools and colleges which are now members of the Friends Council on Education in the United States, more than 20 have been established in the last 25 years. Since a large percentage of the students in most Quaker schools today are non-Quakers, there must be something about such schools which appeals to a wide public.

Throughout my life I have been associated with a number of Quaker schools and colleges. As readers are already aware, I attended Westtown School and Earlham College, both Quaker institutions. Later I taught at Friends Select and Friends Central, day schools in the Philadelphia area. During that time, I also served on the

Education Committee of Philadelphia Yearly Meeting (Arch Street) which worked with several small elementary schools. Later I was on the Board of Managers of Oakwood School in Poughkeepsie, New York, and chairman of its Long-Term Planning Committee. In more recent years I have been on the Schools Committee of the New York Quarterly Meeting of the Religious Society of Friends, a committee which is responsible for Friends Seminary in Manhattan and the Brooklyn Friends School. For brief periods I have been chairman of the committees of both those institutions, during some very difficult periods.

In addition, I have done some writing about Quaker education. Several years ago the Philadelphia Yearly Meeting Committee on Education printed and distributed widely my leaflet on "First Things First: The Case for Friends Schools." At about the same time I spoke to the Sunday morning forum of the Radnor Friends Meeting on "A Friends Community School: A Plan." Those remarks were mimeographed and received an astonishingly wide circulation. Even some of the headmasters of non-Quaker schools obtained that document. Three of them came to talk with me about it and one tried to persuade me to become curriculum director of his new school in Arizona.

Later I wrote the pamphlet "Going to Meeting" and a chapter in my book *Toward a Fourth Century of Quakerism* on "Developing Silent Worshippers." Both are intended primarily for Friends schools.

More recently I have drafted several annual reports on the three Quaker schools with which I have worked as a board member and memoranda on the future of each of those institutions.

300 YEARS OF QUAKER SCHOOLS

In order to think about and plan for Quaker schools in the future, we need from time to time to review the story of Quaker schools over a period of 300 years.

From almost the beginning of the Quaker movement, Friends were interested in the education of their children.

In 1688 George Fox set up two schools, one for boys and one for girls. From then on, Quaker schools were numerous in England. That concern for education grew in part from the fact that the Society of Friends depended upon a lay ministry. Therefore every Friend needed to be educated for "the priesthood of all believers."

It emanated, too, from the belief in a special kind of Quaker community, based upon a unique way of life which was religiously-based. That way of life could be learned in the home, but it also needed to be learned in schools.

Their interest in the education of girls, something radical in those days, was derived from the fact that Friends granted equal rights to women and girls because of their belief that all persons are children of God.

From the earliest times English Quakers were educational pioneers. One was William Penn, who pointed out in his *Advice on Education* that "we are in pain to make them (the students) scholars, but not men." He lamented the fact that the memories of children were pressed too soon, that they learned foreign languages which they would never use, and that their natural interest in mechanical, physical, and natural knowledge was neglected.

Science and nature study were introduced early in English Quaker schools and both have been stressed throughout the 300 years of such institutions. Partly as a result of this, English Friends have been outstanding in those two fields. In fact Ruth Fry pointed out in her book *Quaker Ways* that Quakers produced 46 times the number of Fellows in the Royal Society in England in the period between 1851 and 1900 as the general populace.

Student participation was also encouraged in English Quaker schools, starting with the introduction of the monitorial system by Joseph Lancaster.

In the American colonies, and later, when we became a nation, Friends continued this concern for education. As soon as Quakers moved into a locality, they built a Meeting House and in it school was held. Then a separate building was constructed for the school, almost always next to the Meeting House. And in one of those structures there was a library.

Before compulsory public education became common, there were hundreds of Quaker schools in the United States. For example, there were nearly 100 such schools in Indiana at one time.

Gradually Friends pioneered also in secondary schools or academies. As public secondary education expanded, however, most of those schools were closed or bought by local governments. A few along the Atlantic coast remain today, and several new ones have been founded.

In the 19th century Friends in the United States founded several colleges and all but one of them, Nebraska Central, still exist. In addition, two new ones have been formed in recent years — Malone College in Ohio and the Friends World College in New York.

In every period of our history in this part of the world, some Friends have been educational pioneers. They were among the first to be interested in the education of Indians and then of Negroes. Early they stressed science and several Quakers were among the earliest advocates of manual training. Quakers were also active in the kindergarten movement. And in the progressive education movement Quakers and Quaker schools were prominent. For example, three of the 30 schools in the Eight Year Experiment of the Progressive Education Association were Quaker schools. Many Quakers were active in the movement for free public education, too.

Friends Schools in the U.S.A. Today

In a long period of association with Quaker schools, I have heard many talks, listened to many panels, and taken part in many discussions on "What is a Friends School?" I have also read nearly everything that has been printed in the last 35 years on that theme, and there is now a sizeable collection of such publications. Among the books worthy of special mention are Howard Brinton's *Quaker Education in Theory and Practice,* Douglas Heath's *Humanizing Education,* and Elton Trueblood's *The Idea of a College.* Among the many pamphlets,

mention should be made of John Lester's "The Place of
the Quaker School in Contemporary Education" and his
"Ideals and Objectives of Quaker Education," Douglas
Heath's "Why a Friends School?" and Tom Brown's "A
Theology of Quaker Education."

To the many attempts to define a Quaker school I had
hoped to add my own concise statement here. But I found
that impossible. Instead, I will record the following short
and sometimes overlapping statements which tumbled
out of my mind as I began writing this section:

At best a Friends school is a laboratory for learning the Quaker
way of life — a religious community in the broadest sense of the
word religious.

It is a community in which quality education is prized, but human
excellence is valued even more.

It is a community in which teachers and students are excited about
people, ideas, and things and are beginning to sense that there is
Purpose in every aspect of life.

It is a community in which students explore, examine, probe, and
evaluate selected segments of life suitable to their maturity and
interests, under the guidance of competent and committed
teachers who care about human beings and purposeful living.

It is a community in which boys and girls are exposed to excellence
and greatness — in people, in art, in literature, in science, in
music, and in philosophy.

It is a community in which students and teachers examine
alternatives — in faiths, in life styles, in literature and art and
music and other subjects, in hobbies, and in friends — beginning
to make tentative choices for the rest of their lives.

It is a community in which students and teachers learn to value
themselves and their heritage and in which they are beginning to
value a wide variety of other human beings and their heritages.

It is a community in which students learn to learn.

It is a community in which cooperation rather than competition is
stressed and where the competition encouraged is against oneself.

It is a community in which teachers and students are constantly
examining and clarifying values, making sense out of life,
discovering purpose, meaning, and significance.

It is a community which serves as a home base for explorations into the wider world, including the international community.

It is a community of persons from different backgrounds — racially, religiously, economically, and someday, internationally, searching for similarities and learning to appreciate differences.

It is a non-violent community in which conflicts are resolved peacefully.

It is a community in which simplicity is stressed.

It is a community in which "success" in presently accepted terms is decried and new criteria explored, recalling Mildred Young's comment that "Personal success in the terms of our contemporary culture is no longer a legitimate goal for a Friend."

It is a community in which problems are explored realistically, ranging from personal problems to world-wide issues.

It is a community in which teachers and students are experimenting with new types of education and with the improvement of older types of learning.

It is a community in which the present and future crewmen of our tiny, fragile spaceship EARTH are trained for life well into the 21st century by living creatively NOW.

It is an extended family.

It is people, a place, and a process or processes, all dominated by a Purpose, to serve God through serving the one race to which we all belong — the human race.

Perhaps those statements are too idealistic for some people. To me they are goals or ideals. They may not all be attained, but they should make us all stretch. As Robert Browning said:

> . . .man's reach should exceed his grasp,
> Or what's a heaven for?

Some people may also point out that many of these statements apply as well to public schools as to independent schools, especially Quaker schools. That is true, for much that is good for the students in Friends schools and colleges is good for students in ALL schools. I have no quarrel with public schools. In fact many of the productive years of my life have been devoted to their improvement. I believe deeply in public schools. But I believe in a pluralistic approach to education, as I do to religion and other aspects of life. Therefore I believe in public AND in private education.

However, I believe that Quakerism is a distinctive way of life based on the belief that purposeful living is fundamentally religious. That cannot be the philosophy of public schools, per se. I believe, too, that the Quaker way of conducting business as a group is a superior form of democracy to the voting and majority-minority form of democracy practiced in the United States and in other nations. And the "sense of the Meeting" approach cannot be practiced in public schools because it is based on religious experience. Furthermore, Quakers at their best are adventurers, pioneers, radicals — and public schools by their very nature as institutions responsive to all the people cannot be as flexible, daring, and innovative as Friends Schools, at their best, can be.

There are Friends who believe that the Quaker way of life can be learned in the home and in the various activities provided by the Meeting. Of course that is true. But how much more likely that way of life is to be learned if it is practiced, too, for many hours a day, in a school.

Such schools as I have tried to suggest will not appeal to everyone. But I am convinced that there are people everywhere who want a basically Quaker education for their children and that our Friends schools and colleges need to stress the unique Quaker characteristics of their institutions. Friends schools should be distinctive, unique, and different — or cease to exist.

The type of school I have tried to delineate should appeal to many of today's young people because there is a striking parallel between fundamental Quaker beliefs and some of the emphases of the counter-culture — in simplicity, in stress on the equality of the sexes, in criticisms of the existing socio-economic order, in individualism and in the strengths of groups, in protests against conflicts and wars, and in emphasis upon personal integrity.

There are at least 10 basic beliefs of Friends which should apply to Quaker schools. They include the following:

1. The uniqueness and sacredness of all individuals.

2. The belief that worship is central in lives worth living.

3. The stress on small groups and on decisions made by such groups through Quaker methods.

4. The emphasis upon the equality of all human beings, regardless of race, socio-economic status, religion, sex, culture, or nationality.

5. The centrality of the search for Truth, with a premium placed upon reason and on the special leadings of the Spirit.

6. Simplicity.

7. Positive pacifism and the belief that tensions can be relaxed and conflicts resolved peacefully.

8. Concern for the political, social and economic order and the need to develop in all individuals social awareness, social sensitivity, social concern, and social action.

9. Emphasis upon the interrelatedness of all aspects of living.

10. Accent on openness to experimentation and innovation.

Perhaps these 10 points should be cast in the form of Quaker "queries" and answered one by one by Boards of Trustees and staffs of Quaker schools.

SOME SPECIFIC ASPECTS OF QUAKER SCHOOLS

There are many aspects of Quaker institutions on which I would like to comment at length, but space precludes such lengthy discussion. Therefore I shall confine myself to very brief comments on a wide range of topics, hoping that such brevity does not lead to misrepresentation of my point of view.

Location. Because most students will live out their lives in urban settings, it seems to me that many Quaker schools should be located in or near large cities, where students can use the environment as an exciting laboratory for learning. It is encouraging to me that a few

246

Friends schools in recent years have refused to move from their inner-city locations.

Where schools are removed from the urban setting, they should develop plans for their students to take part in some projects in urban centers or at least plan for frequent visits by students to cities to study selected aspects of these urban centers.

But the students in center-city schools need to have varied experiences, too, through visits to rural areas and through student exchanges with schools in rural settings.

One of my dreams for some of our more isolated boarding schools is for a series of two- or three-week visits by their students to a variety of localities. This would provide students with a broader experiential background and help to relieve the inevitable monotony of boarding school life.

Size. The size of Quaker schools must be dictated by many factors, such as the aims of a particular school, its locality, and the number of so-called grades in it.

A very small, family-like school, like the Meeting School in New Hampshire, has some advantages. On the other hand larger schools can provide much diversity in their student bodies, in their teaching staffs, and in their curricula.

Reflection on the Quaker movement leads me to comment, however, that the Quaker way of living seems to thrive best in small groups. Perhaps this means that some of our larger schools need to curb their tendency to grow larger and concentrate upon the development of small groups inside their larger community.

Quaker School Architecture. Some groups of Friends have developed unique styles of architecture for their Meeting Houses in recent years, either through the purchase of old houses which can be converted into Meetings or through the construction of new, modern, simple structures using glass, open beams, and carpeted floors to add life, warmth, and a quiet atmosphere to these places of worship, work, and fun.

As yet, however, there has been little in the way of a unique Quaker architecture for schools. Instead we tend to replicate the hideous brick factories called public schools.

When I was on the Board of Managers of Oakwood School, we did make a start in something different. Instead of constructing one large boys dorm, we designed small units with an apartment for a faculty family and a bachelor apartment attached to each unit. Then, originally, we cut across grade groupings in assigning boys to each unit. In these ways we tried to create a family atmosphere.

There must be scores of ways in which Quaker ideas about living and about education could be carried out architecturally.

The School Head and His or Her Aides. In any educational institution the head is extremely important. I tend to think that this is even more so in a Quaker school. Of course the needs of different schools differ and a qualified principal or president of one institution is not necessarily a suitable head for another. Also there are different periods in the life of an institution, demanding special qualities of the leader in a given era. To me, however, there are at least five basic qualities for the head of any Quaker educational institution. Stated broadly, such a person should be one who is:

. . .a seasoned, concerned, active Friend, or a person with a very similar philosophy of life and of education.

. . .abreast of and sympathetic to carefully-considered innovations in education, with some ideas of his or her own, plus the ability to utilize the good ideas of other people.

. . .able to work with and communicate with people — students, teachers, parents, alumni, Board members and the Quaker community, and members of the wider community.

. . .marked by broad interests and wide experience.

. . .blessed with the capacity to "turn off" the problems of an institution at appropriate times.

Such persons are difficult to find. They always were and they always will be. Furthermore the times in which we are living and the many demands upon the head of a school seem to call for younger persons now than in the past. Gone are the days when the head of a school was selected at the age of 50 or 60 and remained until he was 70 or 80. Consequently we are going to have to wrestle realistically with the problem of what to do with the heads of schools who are no longer suitable as administrators but who are not old enough to retire.

Most Friends schools tend to limit their search for new leadership to the heads of other Quaker institutions or the assistant heads of other schools. Assistants are often extremely capable, but they are not always successful heads. Increasingly we need to consider Quakers from other independent schools, public schools, and colleges, and even persons who have not been administrators in schools.

Especially in our larger schools and in our colleges, we expect too much of the head. That person is supposed to administer a school, spark new ideas, develop curricula, write and speak, get along with a wide variety of persons, and raise funds. Probably we need to think in terms of an "administrative team" with three or four persons working closely together and complementing each other, although the final control must rest with the principal or president.

The Teachers. A good Friends school needs a staff of teachers who are compassionate, concerned, and committed, as well as competent. Such people are scarce, but they do exist. It may not be possible for an independent school to pay everyone salaries commensurate with his or her worth and in line with public school rates. Therefore a school may need to think in terms of a small nucleus of outstanding teachers who remain for several years. Younger teachers would work with them for two or three years and then move elsewhere. George Walton used such a plan at George School throughout his long and successful career as headmaster and it explains in part the reputation that school acquired.

In any school there ought to be a wide variety of human beings with differing talents and personalities. In that way they can serve as "models" for the variety of students. There ought to be Blacks as well as Whites and hopefully a few persons from other parts of the world. And in every faculty there should be some older people as well as many younger teachers. Every human community needs its "grandparents." At Oakwood School we developed a plan for "Quakers in Residence" and asked Walter and Beulah Mohr, who had just retired from George School after many years there, to serve in that capacity. More recently Colin Bell and Barrington Dunbar have served in somewhat similar capacities in several schools in the Philadelphia area. Such plans have tremendous possibilities for capitalizing upon the wisdom and experience of some of our senior citizens.

Today — and tomorrow — we also need to stress the in-service education of teachers far more than we have done in the past.

The Student Body. In the past most Friends schools have been for the gifted scholastically and for the elite economically. Fortunately we have made some progress in recent years in making our schools more cosmopolitan, especially with the inclusion of more Blacks. But we have a long way to go on this score. If we apply to our schools the Quaker belief that there are extraordinary possibilities even in ordinary people, then we will no longer limit our schools to those who would probably gain a good education without much assistance from adults. A small school with a large percentage of teachers with limited experience cannot possibly provide for a student body with a wide range of abilities, but it ought to be able to provide a wider range than is usually the case now.

The Curriculum. The total staff of any Friends school should constantly be considering changes in the curriculum, even though such work may need to be spearheaded by a small steering committee. And from time to time each school should reexamine its total program to see how it is unique as a QUAKER institution.

Here are a few guidelines which should apply to any school, with emphasis upon areas which are particularly pertinent now:

1. Consideration of the curriculum from kindergarten through the 12th grade as a continuum.

2. Provision for as much individualization as possible, including some independent study in the middle and upper grades.

3. Attention to some large group experiences, such as the use of plays and accent on group singing as used in the Scandinavian Folk Schools.

4. Wide use of the local community as a laboratory for learning.

5. Extensive use of resource persons, exposing students to exciting human beings, with an occasional "day" devoted to such events.

6. A rigorous look at the religious dimensions of the school, including the use of occasional small worship groups.

7. Consideration of year-round programs, but with care that such offerings include variety rather than being an extension into the summer of present nine-month programs.

8. Special individualized programs, patterned after current "senior projects," but not limited to seniors.

9. Attention to the education of the emotions, with special reference to music and art.

10. Emphasis at all levels upon the emerging international community.

11. Concentration of learning to learn — the development of skills.

12. Considerable team-teaching, but with care that teams be self selected.

13. Development of Resource Centers or Learning Centers as an extension of the idea of a school library.

14. Emphasis upon sports in which people can engage throughout their lives.

The General Atmosphere of a School. Those of us who have visited a great many schools feel that we can sense the atmosphere of any institution merely by walking through it with our eyes and ears open. In a superior school the air crackles. One can sense the tone of the school by whether students come early and/or stay late, by how they treat visitors and each other on the playground and in the corridors, by the number of students in the library or resource center and how they are

251

working, and by the atmosphere in the lunchroom. Of course classes should be visited, but it is fascinating to realize how much one can learn about a school without ever going into its classes.

The Board of Trustees or the School Committee. In many independent schools the board is composed solely or largely of businessmen. That usually provides strong financial support for the institution, but it ordinarily deemphasizes concern for the educational aspects of a school or college.

It seems to me that the board or committee of a Friends school should consist of persons representing a wide range of competencies, including persons who are adept in financial matters and those who are experienced in education. All members should be concerned with the "Quakerliness" of the institution.

There may well be some non-Quaker members, especially parents, teachers, and alumni. But they should serve as individuals and not as representatives of any group. Otherwise they become spokesmen for vested interests and that is not the spirit in which Quakers do business. Quaker and non-Quaker parents usually bring strength to a committee or board, but care needs to be exercised that they do not look at the school solely as parents or concentrate on the age group in the school in which their children are enrolled.

It is my strong conviction that students should be consulted from time to time, but that they should not serve on a school committee or board. It is difficult enough for teachers to serve in situations which involve the principal and their colleagues and include confidential matters, let alone asking students to operate in such delicate situations.

All decisions of a Quaker school committee should be arrived at by the "sense of the Meeting" and minutes should be written and approved by the group at the time decisions are made, rather than a month later.

The major task of a board or committee is to determine basic policies and not to concern themselves with the details of running a school. And only in extreme cases should the committee intervene in the hiring and firing of members of the school staff.

In two of the schools with which I have been connected, a very small group from the board meets twice a year with the principal for a rigorous and confidential examination of the relations between the committee and the head of the institution. That is a practice which has proved to be of value to all parties concerned.

Finances. I do not pretend to be an expert in school finances but I have learned a few things in that area in my years on school committees. One is that most schools do not do enough to interpret their programs and problems to their constituencies. If the channels of communication are open, there will be more financial support of the institution. Second, I have learned that small foundations, especially local ones, are too often overlooked in the search for funds. Third, annual giving programs are a must for all independent schools today. And fourth, in larger schools it is essential to have a qualified, full-time person as a fund-raiser and public relations officer, with adequate supporting services for that person.

CONCLUSION

No one knows what the future of independent schools and colleges will be, including Quaker institutions. But I feel that Quaker schools have a distinctive role to play as a special outreach of the Religious Society of Friends. Surely educating mature, intelligent, concerned individuals is as important, or more so, as caring for the broken individuals produced by a sick society.

CHAPTER 18

Semi-Retirement and Retirement — A Lifetime of Learning and Teaching in Retrospect

It is tragic to see how long some people work, even when they do not need to do so. For example, a valued colleague at Brooklyn College, who was not well, hired a neighbor to drive him many miles each day so that he could meet his classes and earn his pension. But he thereby overtaxed himself and died shortly after his retirement.

Relatively early in my career at Brooklyn College, I decided I would retire as soon as I had accumulated 25 years of service, thereby qualifying for a sizeable pension. I calculated that would be in 1971. By that time I would have been at the college 23 years. Two sabbatical years would not count, but I had purchased four years of "prior service," based on teaching elsewhere, and so would meet the required 25 years. Then something unforeseeable happened; the state legislature reneged on its promise to credit "prior service" for pensions. Consequently I had to decide whether to continue teaching for another four years, or retire on a much smaller pension.

Several factors affected my decision. I had already given up my work with student teachers as too strenuous and I felt that the regular courses, without field experience, were not nearly as beneficial. In addition, I had taught most of those courses many years and some of the zest for them was gone even though I felt I was still

255

doing a creditable job. Also, I felt the strain of teaching, writing, traveling, speaking, and working with various organizations. Furthermore, I had serious misgivings about the willingness of the college administration to support adequately our new teacher education program. I also had in mind the Quaker tradition of retiring as early as possible in order to devote oneself to Quaker work and allied activities.

So I went on early retirement in 1971, taking the smaller pension and hoping to supplement it with writing, speaking, and consulting. There was a department party for several of us who retired that year, plus a heart-warming resolution passed by the Education Department and the Faculty Council of the college. And there were several smaller parties given by close friends.

One of the most gratifying experiences shortly after retirement was a banquet in New York City at which the Middle States Council for the Social Studies presented me with the Harry J. Carman Award for distinguished service in the social studies, nationally and internationally. The fact that the award had gone to Margaret Mead the previous year enhanced its value to me.

In the first few years after leaving Brooklyn College I was able to devote considerable time to the top-priority project of the Association for Childhood Education International, called Neighbors Unlimited, and to the UNESCO Associated Schools project in the U.S.A. In addition I traveled on behalf of the Ginn social science textbook series. For some time I served as co-chairman of the joint committee of the National Council for the Social Studies and the Children's Book Council and wrote for the Curriculum Advisory Service in Chicago.

In addition I spent considerable time and energy on the Quaker schools in Brooklyn and in Manhattan.

SOME REFLECTIONS ON A LIFETIME OF LEARNING AND TEACHING

All of us reflect on our lives at many points in our

careers. We are even more likely to do so after we retire. And if we try to record something about our lives in published form, we reflect ever more on what has transpired.

In this process patterns which we have known existed seem even more clear and patterns which we had not discerned seem to emerge. Some readers have probably seen such patterns in the pages they have already read. At this point I should like to make some comments on my observations, aware that such reflections are highly subjective.

In writing this account I have realized even more than before the debt I owe to my family. I have written more about my Grandmother Holloway than about my Kenworthy grandparents, largely because she was a more dramatic and pioneering person. But the influence of my Grandfather and Grandmother Kenworthy was great. My comments on my father have made me realize more than before his influence on my life. I have become aware, for example, of his pioneering stance and of his unique contributions as a midwestern Quaker who was able to build some small but significant bridges between eastern and midwestern Friends. Both my mother and my step-mother contributed significantly, also, to my life in many ways. My stepmother was especially influential in encouraging me to write.

Ours has been a mobile family and that can be disrupting, especially for children. However, we did have a home base and that was the home of our Kenworthy grandparents and the Friends Church in New London, Indiana.

I believe that I have also been fortunate in having had more outstanding teachers than most people have had, a point already mentioned.

And if one believes strongly in the importance of a rich experiential background for purposeful living, then it should be apparent that I have had an unusually large number of such experiences, from my earliest years to the present. Many of them have been provided by my family; others I have sought myself. In several situations I have taken risks, such as the decision to go to Germany in 1940-1941, when some members of my family opposed my going. I believe those risks were worth taking and that some daring is important in life.

Permeating all that I have done has been my Quaker heritage. But it has become more than a heritage; it has become a philosophy of life and a way of living, self-chosen.

In glancing back over my life, three main concerns seem to have dominated it. One was my desire to do everything possible to improve social studies instruction. A second was my keen interest in improving the international dimension of education. The third has been my interest in the revitalization of the Religious Society of Friends.

Probably the most effective work I have done and the parts of my life from which I have derived the most satisfaction have been "frontier jobs," such as the experimental work at Friends Central in the Eight Year Study, my part in the formation of UNESCO, my participation in two efforts at Brooklyn College to improve teacher education, and my pioneering efforts in the field of international education.

My good friend, Jack Niemeyer, the long-time President of Bank Street College in New York City, said publicly once that "If Kenworthy is around, you can be sure that something new, exciting, and significant is happening." That is one of the highest tributes anyone has ever paid to me.

Seldom have I spoken or written specifically on philosophical issues, although I hope that my philosophy of life has permeated everything I have said, written, or done. Perhaps a series of quotations which I read at the Commencement exercises of the Brooklyn Friends School in 1973 will reveal something about my philosophy of life. Here are the quotations I used:

> **The great aim of life is to spend it for something which will outlast it.** William James.

> **To turn all we possess into the channels of universal love becomes the business of our lives.** John Woolman.

I feel that the capacity to care is the thing which gives life its deepest significance. Pablo Casals.

I find that the great thing in life is not where we stand, but the direction in which we are moving. Oliver Wendell Holmes.

I saw that there was an ocean of darkness and death, but an infinite ocean of light and love which flowed over the ocean of darkness. George Fox.

This is the great new problem of mankind. We have inherited a large house, a great world house, in which we have to live together — black and white, Easterner and Westerner, Gentile and Jew, Catholic and Protestant, Moslem and Hindu — a family unduly separated by ideas, cultures, and interests, who, because we can never live apart, must learn somehow to live with each other in peace. Martin Luther King Jr.

It is not incumbent on you to complete the task, but neither is it possible for you to desist from it altogether. Hillel the Elder.

I will be satisfied to furnish just a little mud for the Great Construction. Pierre Ceresole.

You say the little efforts
I make will do no good;
They never will prevail
To tip the hovering scale
Where justice hangs in the balance.
I don't think I
Ever thought they could.
But I am prejudiced
Beyond debate
In favor of my right to choose
Which side shall feel
The stubborn ounces
Of my weight.   Bonaro Overstreet

In a sense one cannot share his experiences with others. Nevertheless I should like to record a few terse comments on some of the things I think I have learned, at least in part. Briefly stated, here are a few such reflections:

The importance of a philosophy of life, a value system, or a religion which is inclusive rather than exclusive and which permeates every aspect of one's life.

The importance of articulating one's philosophy and

sharing it with others, as occasion arises, as well as living it.

The importance of promoting pluralism in all aspects of life — in the social sciences, in religion, in education, and in the U.S.A. as a nation, as well as on the world scale.

The importance of working with groups of people to effect changes, rather than trying to go it alone.

The importance of "timing" in effecting change.

The importance of learning that one will be criticized if he is pioneering. "Do not expect people to help; expect them to throw stones in your path" is what Pierre Ceresole said about such situations. (This has been a difficult lesson for me to learn.)

The importance of priorities in one's life — selecting carefully a few issues with which one wrestles rather than trying to engage in too many organizations or movements.

The importance of learning the interrelatedness of local, national, and international problems.

The importance of expressing appreciation to people rather than limiting one's remarks to criticisms, important as they are at times.

The importance of recognizing the potentialities of people for evil as well as for good, so that one is not just a starry-eyed idealist but a practical idealist.

The importance of planning ahead, wherever possible, or organizing one's life, — and of hard work.

The importance of what Thoreau calls "a broad margin in one's life." (Another lesson which I have had difficulty learning.)

One of the limitations of my life has been the lack of a family of my own. But there have been compensations; many of the things I have done would not have been possible had I had a family.

Throughout this volume I have emphasized some of my

deepest concerns and interests and I have said little about the fun I have had, although much of my work has been fun. The line between work and fun has often been thin or non-existent.

But there have been many other forms of fun, too. My interest in music has been high on such a list, whether it was playing the piano, listening to records, or going to concerts. As I have traveled in various parts of the world, I have "collected conductors" or "collected orchestras" and for many years I have had season tickets to concert series of the New York Philharmonic, the American Symphony, the Great Performers at Lincoln Center, and/or the outstanding series at Brooklyn College. Almost always I have taken a group of friends with me.

Over the years I have seen scores of plays, on and off Broadway, including such outstanding performances as *South Pacific, Death of a Salesman, The Miracle Worker, My Fair Lady, Cat on a Hot Tin Roof, The Young Luther, Victoria Regina,* and *Fiddler on the Roof.*

For many years tennis was my favorite sport.

Obviously reading has been another form of fun. I have read thousands of books. Many of them have been connected with my work; others were merely leisure reading. My favorite forms of reading have been autobiographies, biographies, historical accounts, books about contemporary problems, and books about other countries and peoples.

In recent years my house in Brooklyn, near the college, has been a special pleasure. Although I did not have a large plot of ground, I planned it so that almost all the trees would be flowering or colorful trees — pink and white dogwoods, a Japanese quince, two mountain ashes, a Japanese maple, and a Norway spruce. And my flower garden has been a constant source of pleasure.

Then, too, there have been friends with whom I could share my fun — and my problems.

Of the 65 years to date, the most exciting have probably been the year in Nazi Germany and the nine months spent in visiting the new nations and interviewing their leaders. But all the years have had their excitement and their rewards, as well as their problems and frustrations.

By and large my life has been one of expanding horizons — geographically, religiously, educationally, and politically. It has been a rich and rewarding lifetime of learning and teaching, as well as a lifetime of nudging educators and prodding Quakers in new directions.

And for the future? So long as I have the physical energy and mental awareness, I am certain there will be plenty to do. But there will be many adjustments to make as the years roll by.